UNI... RS

Attitudes, Innuendo, and Regulators

Studies in  Interpretation

Melanie Metzger and Earl Fleetwood, General Editors

Attitudes, Innuendo, and Regulators

Challenges of Interpretation

Melanie Metzger and
Earl Fleetwood, Editors

GALLAUDET UNIVERSITY PRESS

Washington, D.C.

Studies in Interpretation

A Series Edited by Melanie Metzger and Earl Fleetwood

Gallaudet University Press

Washington, D.C. 20002

http://gupress.gallaudet.edu

ISBN 1-56368-322-9

ISSN 1545-7613

Cover design by David Alcorn

Interior design by Rich Hendel

Composition by Alcorn Publication Design

Cover photo by Rex Bavouselt - The University of Iowa.

∞ The paper used in this publication meets the minimum requirements of
American National Standard for Information Sciences—Permanence of Paper
for Printed Library Materials, ANSI Z39.48–1984.

Contents

Introduction

The Studies in Interpretation Series that began in 2003 continues now with volume 2 in 2005. We originally proposed this series of volumes dedicated to empirical research related to interpretation and translation of signed and spoken languages because of the need for a consistent source of data-based information to relate to theoretical and applied aspects of the field for students, practitioners, consumers, researchers, and educators, both as an avenue for sharing information found and for reading the findings of other researchers.

Volume 1 was international in scope, containing chapters devoted to a variety of topics, focusing on both monologic and interactive interpretation of both spoken and signed languages. Volume 2 adds to this eclectic theme, with studies of interpreting from scholars in the United States, the United Kingdom, and Australia. Although volume 2 is divided into two sections like the first volume, it looks at interpreting through a different lens. The first section focuses on working conditions and the second on interpreting practice.

In the section on working conditions, Madden addresses an area often overlooked in the realm of interpretation, and particularly signed language interpretation. Madden's study examines occupational overuse syndrome in signed language interpreters in Australia. She proposes rationale for existing problems as well as possible solutions. Also in this section, Forestal examines another aspect of interpretation that is frequently overlooked: consumers. In his study, Forestal explores attitudes of Deaf leaders toward signed language interpreters. As a growing body of research focuses on interpretation as a discourse process (cf. Wadensjö 1998; Metzger 1999; Roy 2000; and Napier 2003) embedded in social contexts, studies of social perceptions of all stakeholders takes on new meaning. Only by examining the attitudes of social actors in conjunction with the discourse process that constitutes interpretation can we begin to paint a reliable picture of what interpreters do, how to improve professional practice, and how to better prepare students to enter the field.

In the second part of the volume, the focus on interpreting practice includes three chapters that, again, provide international representation. Tray provides an in-depth description of innuendo and its function in interaction. With that, he then outlines his study of the interpretation of innuendo by native and non-native language users as they interpret a source text into American Sign Language. In the remaining chapters, Mather and Harrington focus on interpretation specifically in educational contexts. Mather brings an anthropological lens to her study, providing a useful focus on the role of visually based regulators. She not only provides a description of the ways in which these were employed by interpreters, but also practical recommendations regarding their use by interpreters in mostly hearing, English-based classrooms, Harrington takes a broader focus examining several themes that occur in his study of interpreters in the United Kingdom. In keeping with the spirit of this series, all chapters provide a clearer picture of interpretation resulting from data-based studies and also raise new questions on which future research can focus.

It is our hope that this volume, and subsequent volumes, will support the growth of data-based research in the field of interpretation. As practitioners increasingly find support from agencies in conducting interpreting research and as partnerships in data-collection and analysis are forged, practitioners, researchers, students, and ultimately consumers stand to benefit from gains both in theoretical and applied understanding of our work as it relates to the most practical, everyday aspects of interpretation and translation services.

Thanks are due to many who have made this volume of the series a reality. Thank you to Ivey Wallace and to Deirdre Mullervy for their hard work and for their patience. Thanks also to Valerie Dively, Steven Collins, Risa Shaw, Cynthia Roy, and Karen Malcolm for their time and expertise. Few people are fortunate to have such a warm, talented, and experienced group of colleagues, and for this we are grateful. Thanks also to the students in the Master of Arts in Interpretation program at Gallaudet University for their interest in these topics and in the process of scholarship as it applies to interpretation. Appreciation is also due those who contributed to this volume and to the interpreters and consumers who were willing to participate in their research. Without such valuable resources, we could not extend our understanding of what we do. Finally, thank you Eric and Jill for patiently reading drafts and providing comments, and to Dawson for his unbelievable patience and joyful help in making this volume possible.

Melanie Metzger
Earl Fleetwood,
Series Editors

Part I **Working Conditions**

The Prevalence of Occupational Overuse

Syndrome in Sign Language Interpreters

in Australia—What a Pain!

Maree Madden

Occupational health and safety (OHS) issues have been the focus of much discussion and research over the past two decades. Attention has been given to the effects of exposure to environmental factors such as heat, noise, dust, and vibration; physical factors such as workstation design (Moore, Wells, & Ranney, 1991); the length of time spent on tasks (Waersted & Westgaard, 1991); mental factors such as stress and depression (Kurppa, Viikari-Juntura, Kuosma, Huuskonen, & Kivi, 1991), and work organization factors, such as shift length, which affect injury propensity (Williams, 1988); as well as the impact of payment systems on injury incidence (Mayhew & Quinlan, 1998). Among the outcomes of such research have been recommendations for redesign of the work process or workplace; care for and education of workers in order to assist in retaining or regaining health; redesign of work practices; programs to reduce the likelihood of recurrent injury or illness; and changes in legislative requirements for workplace health and safety.

The occupational group examined in this study was composed of Australian Sign Language interpreters. This group had not previously been examined in terms of its workplace health status or for specific health and safety threats from their work. This lack of attention may be because the emergence of signed language interpreting as a profession has been comparatively recent. Until approximately 20 years ago, paid signed language interpreting was mainly performed by individuals whose primary role was that of welfare worker or counselor for members of the Deaf community. Much voluntary or underpaid interpreting was also done by family members or friends of the Deaf person involved. These "interpreters" often undertook interpreting duties ignorant of their OHS rights and responsibilities, without knowledge of an interpreting code of ethics, and usually without support and development mechanisms such as accreditation schemes, training programs, professional associations, or even peer support.

Two other reasons that may account for the lack of research into signed language interpreting in Australia are:

1. The field is a comparatively small one (the total number of accredited practitioners in Australia numbered only 165 at the time of this research (NAATI, 1991); and
2. The field is largely populated by women (129 of the 165 indicated above are women); a group whose paid and unpaid work has historically been considered of secondary importance to that of men.

THE WORK OF SIGNED LANGUAGE INTERPRETERS IN AUSTRALIA

Since 1982, examination and accreditation of professional signed language interpreters in Australia has been conducted by the National Accreditation Authority for Translators and Interpreters (NAATI). NAATI examines and accredits interpreters and translators in Australia in a broad range of spoken languages.

NAATI offers five levels of accreditation: (i) language aide: for individuals who use another language while performing other duties (e.g., a clerk employed by the Australian Taxation Department who may interview clients in another language and keep notes of the interview in English); (ii) paraprofessional interpreter: for people for whom interpreting forms a minor part of other duties. This level of accreditation is intended for use in relatively straightforward interpreting situations; (iii) interpreter: the basic professional level, intended for individuals who work full-time in the community, health, welfare, legal, and education fields; (iv) advanced interpreter: the level of accreditation for a simultaneous conference interpreter; and (v) senior advanced interpreter: a small group of senior conference interpreters, currently composed only of members of the International Association of Conference Interpreters (AIIC).

NAATI currently offers testing and accreditation at two levels in Australian Sign Language—paraprofessional interpreter and interpreter.

NAATI is not directly involved in the education of signed language or spoken language interpreters, although it oversees the approval of courses, monitors institutions which offer training courses, and coordinates moderation of examinations in these courses.

While interpreter training at a professional level has been available for several spoken languages since the mid-1970s in Australia, training in Australian Sign Language (Auslan) interpreting has only so far been achieved at the paraprofessional level (Ozolins & Bridge, 1999, p. 16). At the time of writing, training courses for paraprofessional Auslan interpreters have been offered in Victoria, Tasmania (once only), South Australia, Queensland (once only), New South Wales (NSW), and Western Australia. These courses are offered at colleges and institutes of technical and further education [TAFE]. Entry requirements, course duration, content, and exit qualifications can vary widely between institutions, and there is no requirement for an individual to complete a training program before commencing paid work as an interpreter. In order to improve the quality of training courses, a revised curriculum, to standardize paraprofessional interpreter training course delivery nationally, was approved for use in TAFE colleges and institutes in 1994 and has been in use since then. Discussions concerning national coordination of training courses at the interpreter level commenced in 1993. As of the middle of 2003, only one NAATI accredited course is on offer anywhere in Australia, which provides for training to this higher level for signed language interpreters. There is currently no accreditation or training course for signed language interpreters in Australia at the advanced interpreter level.

Owing to the scarcity of full-time signed language interpreting positions currently available in Australia, many interpreters gain most of their income from part-time or freelance work. Employment in such situations without the benefits of regular work, secure income, and contact with peers tends to make the occupation a solitary one. Further, signed language interpreters are not represented by a single union, although signed language interpreters in Australia may choose to take out membership of a local branch of the Australian Sign Language Interpreters' Association (ASLIA). However, ASLIA is currently more of a support network, rather than of a professional organization with the ability to influence decisions about interpreters' working conditions. The Executive Committee of ASLIA, both nationally and in state branches, is composed of officers who hold honorary positions and must balance their paid work commitments with the work required to achieve the association's aims.

This lack of coordinated institutional support creates difficulties in obtaining recognition of workers' rights, the promotion of the job as a profession, protection of OHS status, and even in the distribution of preventive OHS information. This difficulty was commented upon by interpreters interviewed during this study.

Interpreting is a difficult mental task. It requires the interpreter to deal with two quite different languages simultaneously. Signed language interpreters also exert considerable physical effort in performing their work. Whether interpreting from spoken English into Auslan (voice-to-sign interpreting) or from Auslan into spoken English (sign-to-voice interpreting), intense concentration is required of the interpreter. This process has the capacity to produce significant fatigue after a short time.

An interesting feature of the work of signed language interpreters is that they may spend a large proportion of their working days functioning in their second language. Many interpreters work in predominantly voice-to-sign mode, interpreting the spoken English utterances of a presenter into sign language. In the case of sign-to-voice interpreting, the signed language interpreter speaks in English what the Deaf person has signed. The tendency for most interpreting work to be voice-to-sign mode means that much of an interpreter's working day, and indeed their career, is spent functioning in a language and modality that are not part of their primary communication channel. Given that much interpreting work is also performed in isolation (without another interpreting colleague), it would seem that this type of work would have significant effects on the interpreter's feelings of estrangement and detachment from the self, not to mention the capacity to produce extreme fatigue in a short period of time.

Estrangement and detachment from the products of one's labor have previously been documented for workers in automated plants and assembly-line production, where the speed of processing the product is machine controlled. One of the interpreters in this study made a written comment on the questionnaire form about feeling detached and depersonalized at the end of the day: "*[A negative is] not having the opportunity to voice my thoughts and opinions*" (I 44). Some other interpreters in this study commented during interview that isolation was a negative feature of their work.

Detachment from the process and product of the interpreter's labor is actively practiced and reinforced through the ethics of impartiality and professional distance. Because of requirements for strict adherence to the ethics of confidentiality and impartiality, the content of the service they provide (their product) is not discussed by either employers or colleagues. The code of ethics to which signed language interpreters adhere sets out the conditions under which they must operate. While in the role of interpreter, they function as conduits or channels to communication (and as such, have no stake in the interaction), and none of the information to which they become privy is to be discussed with any other person. The subordination of the interpreter is achieved through referring to him or her as a conduit or a channel; as a means to an end.

The extent of subordination and control is beginning to change as larger numbers of signed language interpreters work on a freelance basis, accepting direct bookings for assignments from a number of different employers at their own discretion. Many interpreters are also beginning to question the requirement of codes of ethics to remain entirely impartial. For example:

> In America the pendulum has swung back [to] the interpreter is an interpreter, full stop, and doesn't want to accept any responsibility for the client. I've seen the "machine model" in America ... It didn't quite hit a peak in Australia, because cautions were expressed. Several of us were aware of the "machine model" and cautioned people against it. There is still a place in human services for recognising that they are dealing with human beings. We are not shorthand machines, we are not typewriters, we are not just a computer for conveying one word into another: that is not our task. I think interpreting goes beyond that. (I 80, male signed language interpreter, employed on a full-time basis)

Interpreters who hold such opinions feel that they should be more involved in the interpreting situation, as a cultural as well as linguistic bridge between the two parties. That is, many interpreters reject the subordination of their mental capacities and the subjugation of their labor to being "a cog in a machine." However, the feelings described above cannot be easily resolved on the job due to the isolated nature of signed language interpreting work and the difficulties that interpreters face in finding opportunities to network with colleagues.

The application of modern management techniques involving team work and high-trust relationships in the interpreting field has been extremely limited. Most interpreters do not have a clearly defined career path, supported by comprehensive and meaningful performance management and provision of structured learning opportunities. While there are general distinctions between work tasks and pay rates for paraprofessional interpreters and higher qualified interpreters, there are no formal, accredited programs in place to assist in skill development.

Organizations have either attempted to obtain the same quantity and quality of output from fewer workers or have created alternative employment arrangements that retain workers on an as-needed basis (Caudron, 1994, p. 52). These responses are demonstrated in two major trends, one being downsizing and restructuring (Beard & Edwards, 1995, p. 109) and the other involving alternative employment arrangements, such as the use of contingent workers (Pfeffer & Baron, 1988, p. 258).

Contingent work is defined as "any job in which the individual does not have an explicit or implicit contact for long-term employment or one in which the minimum hours of work can vary in a non-systematic way" (Polivka & Nardone, 1989, p. 11). The key features of contingent work are the lack of ongoing employment and the low expectation of future employment (i.e., low job security), not the total number of hours worked or the duration of any particular work assignment (Beard & Edwards, 1995, p. 110). Contingent workers may receive no workers' compensation benefits or sick leave entitlements and have few opportunities for advancement with the employing organization (Lansbury & Kitay, 1997, p. 230). All the interpreters interviewed during this study who were employed on a casual or freelance basis commented that provisions such as paid sick leave, recreation leave, superannuation, and workers' compensation were nonexistent for them. Such variation in employment conditions clearly locates signed language interpreters in the secondary labor market, primarily because of the lack of tenure, career progression, union representation, sick leave, recreation leave and workers' compensation entitlements, and the intermittent nature of their work.

Signed language interpreters can clearly be defined as contingent workers, particularly when employed in the education sector, such as in universities and TAFE, where the amount and nature of interpreting work varies depending upon teaching schedules and lecture timetables. Very few interpreters in this study reported that they held a full-time or tenured position (e.g., only 26% of the subjects who completed the questionnaire were employed on a full-time basis). A great deal of employment variety was reported by interpreters in this study.

The requirement for multi-skilling is a feature of signed language interpreting work, as the interpreter's workday may be composed of assignments in a number of settings as varied as educational, legal, and medical. Interpreters interviewed for this study commented on multi-skilling in the following ways:

> The nature of assignments has changed a lot. We're now getting a hell of a lot more work for interpreting in education, and employment training settings.... That has changed the nature of the work a lot. It used to be more the small interpreting—meetings were a rare event. Skills need to be probably a bit more polished than they were. (I 139, male signed language interpreter, employed on a freelance basis)

> Court work [is challenging]. Overall, it is the content and excitement of being involved in something like that. You are just there as the interpreter and when you are trying to get all the bits and pieces from the Deaf client, it's almost like a jigsaw puzzle. (I 118, male signed language interpreter, employed on a full-time basis)

SIGNED LANGUAGE INTERPRETERS AND THEIR LABOR PROCESS

Signed language interpreters do not, in the main, enjoy control over their work. Their work is mostly planned and managed by an employing organization or body, be it a school, tertiary educational institution, local Deaf Society, or community organization. Interpreters are deployed on the basis of demand for their services, and the interpreter's work is often dictated by the number of interpreting assignments scheduled on any given day.

In some (but not all) cases, the person responsible for deciding on the structure of an interpreter's workday is not a qualified interpreter, but rather an administrative clerk with no real understanding of the complexity of the interpreter's work. These administrators are employed by organizations to ensure that the maximum number of interpreting assignments are completed each day, leading to high levels of billable hours of work and maximum revenue for the organization. The pre-conditions for degradation of work are set.

There are no standards for working conditions or agreed-upon expectations, and no guidelines for reporting structures exist. The employment relationship varies widely, depending upon the circumstances of the employment contract or agreement between the interpreter and whoever the employer happens to be. Factors such as recruitment procedures, training provisions (both at the time of hiring and in-service), promotion prospects (or lack of them), and pay levels are not standardized. Therefore, an interpreter may often find him- or herself in the position of negotiating a different set of employment conditions at the commencement of each interpreting assignment.

In situations which are deemed to be emergencies, or when the interpreting requirement cannot be deferred (e.g., a high-level meeting of many participants or a university lecture), the demands or perceived needs of the consumers are deemed to be of greater importance than the interpreter's needs, and work schedules are constructed accordingly. This is, of course, not the case for an interpreter who works on a purely freelance basis, as he or she has control over the structure of the working day and can choose to accept some assignments and reject others.

Interpreters have been further affected recently by the trend of deployment agencies to reduce the size of their interpreting pool, and by decentralized booking services (i.e., bookings for different types of interpreting work are handled by various agencies, rather than one central organization). In any given week, most interpreters work across a wide range of employment settings, which may vary greatly in their complexity. Although demarcation guidelines exist between what can be expected of an accredited interpreter and a paraprofessional interpreter, in reality these lines become blurred owing to the high demand for services. As a result, a paraprofessional interpreter may find her- or himself working in situations ranging from a medical appointment to a university lecture to a police interview in the course of a week, as maximum output is extracted from the interpreter to satisfy the need for profit. There are no language-specific courses on offer anywhere in Australia for signed language interpreters to attend in order to develop the language sophistication required to deal with such a broad range of employment situations.

The flexible specialization theory of up-skilling for employees not only increases reliance upon contingent labor, but also marginalizes gender considerations, in that the conception of *skill* relates to male-based technologies, where skilled workers obtain increased job autonomy (Williams & Thorpe, 1992, p. 41). So-called "women's work" does not generally involve the same level of decision-making or independent planning compared with men's work and allows less freedom for self-regulation, is more repetitive, and is more restricted in space and time (Williams & Thorpe, 1992, p. 42). For example, women are still overwhelmingly concentrated in occupations such as secretary, retail sales clerk, preschool and primary school teacher, waitress, and nurse—all occupations regarded as women's work—derived from the domestic division of labor.

The critique outlined above is particularly relevant for signed language interpreters. One of the reasons that working conditions of signed language interpreters in Australia have not become more secure may be the fact that the majority of interpreters in this country are women. Most interpreters do not enjoy a great deal of autonomy in their working arrangements. Managers of interpreting services are frequently not themselves accredited interpreters, and their focus is on satisfaction of market demand in the most efficient manner, rather than on the skill development of interpreters in their employ, as many interpreters in this study remarked.

Work intensification has certainly been an increasing part of an Australian signed language interpreter's experience over the past decade. As greater numbers of Deaf people gain access to enhanced educational and employment opportunities, the demand for skilled interpreters has rapidly outstripped supply. This dire shortage has meant that the few qualified interpreters who are able to do this work are required by employers to increase their workload to meet demand.

Where employment is by contract, the terms and conditions are usually individually negotiated between the interpreter and employer. Signed language interpreters' only real bargaining tool is that they possess highly demanded and marketable skills, and even this is undermined by a general lack of understanding of the job they do. A number of the interpreters in this study commented on the low perceptions and expectations that clients have of their skills and the value of the work they do. In regard to the expectations of Deaf people, comments included:

I feel sometimes, that the Deaf consumers don't understand what an interpreter physically has to do to interpret. Maybe there could be some sort of training course that goes seven or eight hours a day for three or four days a week. The Deaf people often don't understand the drain that can be on an interpreter. (I 3, female signed language interpreter, employed on a part-time basis)

I think there are some Deaf people who really don't understand what an interpreter is trying to do. They sort of expect you to be perfect and expect that they will understand everything you say. Sometimes Deaf people are intolerant. (I 140, female signed language interpreter, employed on a freelance basis)

In regard to the expectations of hearing (non-Deaf) people:

As long as some communication happens, they're not really too concerned about you. They expect though that one can go on ad infinitum, and they're ignorant on the whole on the need for interpreters, or even what interpreting entails. So they're not considerate of the break and the need to stand up and stretch and that you have to stop for about five minutes. (I 2, female signed language interpreter, employed on a full-time basis)

It always stuns me that people like doctors or teachers . . . know so little about it and start talking straight to me . . . I can't believe what they don't know. A lot of them are completely useless, they have no idea at all, but the other half of them think "God she's clever, look at the way she moves her fingers" even if you're doing the worst job in the whole world. (I 129, female signed language interpreter, employed on a part-time basis)

These comments indicate the lack of understanding and value placed on the work of signed language interpreters. These client attitudes are, in many cases, mirrored by employer attitudes and help in part to explain why signed language interpreters are part of a devalued group of employees (i.e, why they are part of the peripheral labor market).

As a group of predominantly self-employed individuals, who work on a freelance or subcontractor basis, signed language interpreters have always lacked labor market power or union representation. Their work is usually on a payment by results basis, meaning that if an interpreting job is canceled, the interpreter does not receive payment, or may, in some cases, receive a minimum two-hour payment. In most cases, a 24-hour cancellation rule is applied (i.e., if the job is canceled with a day's notice, no payment is made).

As described earlier, there are only two levels of accreditation for signed language interpreters in Australia, and there is very little scope for career advancement. Those interpreters who may benefit from incremental pay, multiskilling, dispute resolution policies and procedures, and variety of working hours are the few who are employed on a full-time basis. In this study, 40 of the 106 questionnaire respondents stated that they were employed on a full-time basis. Further analysis of their employment showed that 12 of these 40 (30% of the full-time employed interpreters and 11% of the total subject pool of 106) were employed in another capacity (e.g., as a coordinator of interpreting services or a teacher of the deaf), leaving only 28 (26% of total respondents) who were employed full-time as an interpreter. Of the remaining 66 respondents, 38 (36%) were employed on a part-time basis, 24 (23%) were employed on a casual or freelance basis, and four (4%) were not currently working.

There are no nationally agreed rates of pay for signed language interpreters in Australia, and only as recently as 1997 was a standardized contract of employment and other employment-related policies formulated and distributed by the Australian Sign Language Interpreters' Association (ASLIA). However, given the informal volunteer nature of this association, the policy documents comprise sets of guidelines only, as ASLIA has no industrial power to develop and promulgate an interpreters' award. There is no compulsion or obligation for either employers or interpreters to adhere to the guidelines in the policy documents. However, during late 1998 and early 1999, at least one consumer organization, the Australian Association of the Deaf, which regularly employs interpreters, has used the contract template to develop employment agreements with individual interpreters.

Given the frequently competitive and sometimes sporadic nature of freelance interpreting, there may be a tendency for one interpreter to undercut another in order to secure an assignment. This undercutting could be in the form of pay rates, but also may encompass the hours per day or number of days per week the interpreter is prepared to work. The cost of interpreters is also an incentive for employers to look for cheaper alternatives such as teacher aides, note-takers or volunteers, friends, and helpers (particularly in the education sector) (Ozolins & Bridge, 1999, p. 54). The fluctuation in working hours, the isolation of the work, and the lack of cohesion and representation for interpreters all contribute to the precarious nature of their employment.

In industries where subcontracting has become the norm, insecurity is a major concern for both employees and self-employed workers (Mayhew, Quinlan, & Bennett, 1996, p. 128). Outsourcing and subcontracting have a significant effect on the labor process, through fragmenting and marginalizing the labor force. Such fragmentation reduces possibilities for workers to interact with each other, thereby reducing the ability to coordinate preventative action on OHS issues. Labor process changes have led to a situation where the potential to organize workers en masse becomes more and more difficult (Williams & Thorpe, 1992, p. 246). Widespread use of outsourcing and subcontracting creates serious OHS concerns.

OCCUPATIONAL HEALTH AND SAFETY CONSEQUENCES OF INCREASED OUTSOURCING AND CASUALIZATION

The trend towards casualization and contract employment has occupational health consequences because working conditions and nonwage benefits which are associated with permanency (sick leave, holiday pay, long service leave, special leave, workers' compensation cover, etc.) do not always or even usually apply to casual workers. It is implicitly recognized that provision of such conditions contribute to the overall health of workers (Heiler, 1994, p. 23). The casuals may therefore find it difficult to change their days of work or take time off when they are ill or stressed. Thus, Heiler concludes, the absence of paid leave for a growing proportion of workers (many of whom are already lowly paid) is a serious health issue (Heiler, 1994, p. 23). The lack of paid sick or recreation leave was commented on by some of the interpreters in this study.

Further, Mayhew (1996, p. 162) argues that subcontractors tend to face an increased number of hazards on worksites compared with employees. They face these hazards for greater periods of time, and because of the intensification of their labor through speed ups, are less able to implement protective practices in their labor process. Such subcontractors, contractors, and consultants are increasingly burned out, and suffer in a somewhat hidden way so that both their productivity and general health suffer (Shatzkin, 1978, quoted in Mayhew, 1996, p. 163). In other words, the proliferation of part-time, casual, and subcontract work in the absence of trade unions and OHS activity is highly likely to compromise OHS outcomes (Brosnan & Underhill, 1998, p. 1; Heiler, 1996, p. 159).

The difficulties in recognizing injury, receiving accurate diagnosis, and securing support from the employer are described in comments made by some of the interpreters in this study.

As recently as 10 years ago, most employment for a freelance signed language interpreter in a capital city would have come predominantly from the local Deaf Society. The interpreter would register with the Deaf Society and would then be contacted for a booking as interpreting assignments became available. This, however, was a far-from-optimal working arrangement, as the shortage of qualified interpreters meant that a few people were given the task of undertaking a high number of assignments per day and per week. The nature of assignments ranged in content from work interviews, to births or ante-natal classes, to marriage ceremonies, to funerals, to union meetings for Deaf employees in a workplace, and to medical appointments and ranged in length from as little as 20 minutes to as much as several hours.

Over the past five to 10 years, a number of alternative specialist interpreter booking agencies have been established in many states of Australia. In both Victoria and New South Wales, state services and private agencies have become significant providers of Auslan interpreters over the past decade. In New South Wales, the change has come about because the Deaf Society of New South Wales made a deliberate policy decision to mainstream Auslan interpreting services and sees itself as providing a residual language service for needs not catered for by mainstream organizations (Ozolins & Bridge, 1999, p. 35). For example, much of the signed language interpreting for health-related issues in public hospitals and community health centers in New South Wales is no longer booked via the Deaf Society, but rather through the Health Care Interpreter Service (HCIS). Interpreting for criminal legal matters and administrative requirements in state government departments is coordinated by the NSW Ethnic Affairs Commission (EAC). The Deaf Society of New South Wales still provides interpreting services for civil legal matters, private medical appointments, financial services, meetings at work and "events of special significance" (such as funerals) (Ladd, 1999, personal correspondence). There are also eight private agencies in New South Wales providing interpreting services for a range of situations.

Such diversification means an interpreter who wishes to do a variety of interpreting work may register with a long list of different deployment agencies in the one city. Thus there has been an increased tendency to outsourcing on the part of the Deaf Societies in the larger cities, rather than the use of staff interpreters. The interpreter then juggles the various assignments, which may come his or her way in order to make a living. It is argued that the health and safety of signed language interpreters has been compromised through such intensification of such work.

Training in injury/illness prevention has not been provided in a coordinated way for signed language interpreters. Interpreters in this study generally commented that their knowledge and understanding of OHS risks came largely through information from colleagues, via workshops arranged by the interpreting association, or through contact with health professionals such as physiotherapists (often in the context of receiving treatment for an injury). Some interpreters commented that their knowledge of the subject had come from their own research into Occupational Overuse Syndrome (OOS). In other words, there appears to be little acceptance of responsibility on the part of employers to provide training and information on OHS for interpreters.

Nichols (1997, p. 102) states that the salience of safety to corporate decision-makers may also vary depending upon the following: whether the organization has high visibility, whether a poor safety record threatens the existence of the enterprise (or of the local community), and whether failure to comply with standards may be perceived as a threat to a valued company image. In the case of major employers of signed language interpreters, that is, state Deaf Societies, the above factors are not particularly influential. Deaf Societies and other deployers of signed language interpreters (with the possible exception of the EAC in New South Wales and the Victorian Interpreting and Translating Service) are not typically high-profile enterprises or overly concerned with the public perception of their work processes. In real terms, many employers of interpreters have shown a poor safety record for some time (as evidenced by comments from respondents in this study), and this poor record does not appear to have threatened their existence. Arguably, one reason for this limited recognition is that OOS patterns among interpreters have not previously been documented. Pressure on interpreters to complete the allocated assignments is kept up by the employer, while it is left up to each interpreter to work out how to cope. For example,

> Something I didn't face three years ago was having to rush from one job to another because there are so many demands. And that's a different challenge I think, coping with the fact that we are now working so many hours a day. Your day is full because there is extra work and

that may lead to problems too, of how to cope with that stress. (I 147, female signed language interpreter, employed on a casual basis)

Well it's like you've got a ten o'clock appointment and a ten-thirty appointment and the ten o'clock appointment is going too long and "Oh hell, are you going to make it to the ten-thirty appointment?" So you jump in the car and you tear off and make it there. And also we're getting more higher level at university and those situations which are really stressful. They really are high stress situations, and we're getting more of them, and we're expected to perform those for two hours or more, which is crazy. Well, that never happened before, we just never had those jobs, and if you did it was talked about for a few weeks beforehand. (I 136, female signed language interpreter, employed on a part-time basis)

As the majority of the signed language interpreters surveyed are women (129 of the 165 interpreters registered at the time of this study), the next section will examine the gender division of labor and the development of the concept of *women's work* in more depth. As a lead-in to this discussion, the next section will be an overview of the position of women in the secondary labor market and some of the forms in which occupational segregation takes place.

GENDER AND WORK

Much of the belief about what constitutes "women's work" and "men's work" stems from the gender division of domestic labor; that is, most of the primary home and childcare responsibilities in our society were historically placed with women. When women moved into paid employment, they typically performed tasks derived from their "normal" domestic duties (e.g., women workers are overrepresented in nursing, childcare, primary school teaching, secretarial, cleaning, and flight attendant positions). Men have traditionally been employed in trade areas such as carpentry and mechanics, and in more technical or scientific areas such as engineering and medicine. This gender differentiation of employment options is known as the sexual or gender division of labor.

In pre-industrial Europe, the household or the family was the basic economic unit, and women's work was both essential and taken for granted. There was no attempt to distinguish between what we have come to call domestic work and paid work (Probert, 1990, p. 74). Women labored not only on the farm, but at all sorts of other work, depending in part on what was available to them. In most areas, their activity was an extension of their household functions of food provision, animal husbandry, and making clothing. They raised chickens as well as children, worked in the fields, made soap, preserved food, and cooked for farmhands. All these tasks were considered to be part of the status of the housewife (Epstein, 1987, p. 25).

Scott and Tilly (1978) note that, like their rural counterparts, urban working-class women contributed to the family economy by tending vegetable gardens, raising animals, and marketing the surplus. In urban households, the entire family was often expected to work (laundering, tailoring, shoemaking, baking, etc.), and parents willed their shops and their clientele to their daughters as frequently as to their sons (Probert, 1990, p. 74). Some women set up cafes in their homes; others sold the food and beverages they had prepared (Scott & Tilly, 1978, p. 104). Many took a job to bring in an additional income (Forrest, 1973, p. 151). They worked as domestics, laundresses, seamstresses, innkeepers, and beasts of burden—hauling heavy loads many times a day. Work of this type was a traditional way of supplementing the family income, and as a result women usually had a great deal of power within the family.

The importance of the mother within the family economy was immense; her death or incapacity could cause a family to walk the line between poverty and destitution (Hufton, 1971, p. 92). The indispensable role of women was demonstrated, too, by the fact that in many communities, widows could manage a farm alone (with the assistance of a few hired hands), whereas widowers found the task almost impossible (Scott & Tilly, 1978, p. 105).

The Industrial Revolution radically transformed these earlier patterns of work. The rise of the factory meant that less and less economic activity occurred around the home, and the home itself was transplanted from a rural to an urban setting (Probert, 1990, p. 74). Large-scale commercial agriculture and the increase in the numbers of factories meant that the family ceased to be an independent productive unit. In working-class families, the Industrial Revolution resulted in a decline in the father's control, along with the potential for a life outside the family for women. This brought a kind of freedom for working-class women, but in so doing it deprived them of a definite work role and status, enforcing a new kind of dependency, which made it necessary for them to sell their labor power outside the family (Pennington & Westover, 1989, p. 1). From the very beginning of paid work outside the family production unit, men and women were in no way equal. The view that marriage was the primary goal for women and that once married, women were supported socially, politically, and financially, was enshrined in law in the nineteenth century. For example, until the Married Women's Property Act of 1884 was passed, married women had no right to own property (Summers, 1994, p. 404; Probert, 1990, p. 75; Pennington & Westover, 1989, p. 6). A woman's property became her husband's on marriage, as did her earnings, and he could dispose of them as he liked whether they lived together or not (Summers, 1994, p. 403).

The belief that women should be confined solely to child-rearing and housekeeping developed during this process of industrialization and the rise of the middle class (Grint, 1991, p. 215; Probert, 1990, p. 91). Middle-class values assigned the husband the role of breadwinner and the wife that of domestic manager (Scott & Tilly, 1978, p. 97). A rigid separation developed throughout industrialized society: Life was divided into public and private spheres, and the work opportunities of men and women were polarized (Grint, 1991, p. 71). Women ceased to be the food providers, the bread makers, and the concept of men as the bread-*winner* emerged (Novarra, 1980, p. 33, original emphasis). A wife who stayed at home was a status symbol in Victorian times, indicating the husband's high earning capacity (Pennington & Westover, 1989, p. 2; Pahl, 1984, p. 34).

The type of work that women and men do has become very different. The perception of typical women's work is that it is usually indoor work, considered to be lighter than men's work. It is clean, safe, physically undemanding, often repetitive and considered monotonous or boring, requires dexterity rather than skill, often has domestic associations, and is emotionally sensitive and nurturing (Fine, 1992, p. 74). Women are portrayed as good at handling people, at training, and at routine administration (Bradley, 1999, p. 79). Women's work tends to lack mobility and is tied to a particular workstation; it is labor-intensive and may well have associations and requirements of beauty and glamour (Beechey, 1987, p. 126; Scott, 1984, p. 62; Game & Pringle, 1983, p. 9).

By contrast, men's work is associated with the outdoors, with strength and physicality. Men's work may be heavy, dirty, and dangerous. It is often highly mobile and requires skill and training (Sayer & Walker, 1992, p. 52; Beechey, 1987, p. 127; Game & Pringle, 1983, p. 9). Men are portrayed as being good with figures, machinery, and decision-making

(Bradley, 1999, p. 79). Men's work is frequently highly technical, based on mechanical knowledge or scientific expertise; and it is emotionally detached (Fine, 1992, p. 73). At the highest level, it requires the characteristics of creativity, innovation, intelligence, responsibility, authority, and power (Game & Pringle, 1983, p. 9; Novarra, 1980, p. 28).

Even as Western society is at the beginning of the twenty-first century, in a world far removed from that of the Industrial Revolution, stereotyped notions of appropriate gender roles persist; and in fact, the ideologies surrounding the roles seem to have nearly as strong a hold as ever. These conventions spring from the link to biological reproductive function, which has, for many centuries, legitimated the assignment to women of the major responsibility for childcare and domestic labor (Bradley, 1999, p. 29). In addition, there are other arguments which assert that men and women have different intellectual and emotional qualities, and that these are biologically determined.

In investigating the employment of women then, we are studying a subject that highlights the oppression of women in a society which has institutionalized the concept of dependency (Pennington & Westover, 1989, p. 13; Fowlkes, 1987, p. 4). When women move into the wage labor sphere, they often perform commercialized forms of the same activities, which center on the care and servicing of other people and their needs, such as the cleaning, preparation, and serving of food; making clothing; nursing; and primary teaching (Bradley, 1999; Probert, 1990, p. 73; Grint, 1991, p. 33). That is, women's paid work roles are derived from their place in the domestic division of labor.

One of the difficulties for women's participation in the work force is that both management and labor process writers have tended to define *skill* in very conventional terms, in relation to the characteristics of *male* craft labor (Probert & Wilson, 1993, p. 52; Peitchinis, 1989(a), p. 59 [original emphasis]). Men define the meaning of key terms such as *skill, merit, competence* and *value*. They decide what is meant by *quality* and *excellence,* setting the rules for their measurement and evaluation and, crucially, determining the level of economic rewards (Bradley, 1999, p. 189). Women's labor (no matter how much technical dexterity, mental expertise, or training it requires) is usually defined as inferior simply because it is women's labor (Probert & Wilson, 1993, p. 52; Beechey, 1987, p. 127). Thus early childhood teaching (usually performed by women) is generally revered but rewarded less than is secondary school science teaching (more often performed by males). While women sew, men become designers, women cook and men are chefs, women nurse and men become medical professionals.

Scott (1984) believes that the most important distinguishing feature of women's work, in the home and in paid employment, is that it is labor-intensive. These types of work share a requirement for relatively large numbers of people to undertake them.

> There are many operations [especially in service industries] that have proved difficult or expensive to mechanise. The same is true of caring for children, making beds, cleaning house, cooking for a family. Since productivity is low, labour costs must be kept low. It is important that women continue to do the jobs in the home free because they are labour-intensive. Labour-intensive jobs are reserved for women outside the home just because women can be paid less (Scott, 1984, p. 62).

Signed language interpreting is one such labor-intensive job, which is frequently performed by women (of the 106 subjects in this study, 81 (76%) are women). Language interpretation generally is an area that has proved to be difficult to mechanize because of the intricacies of languages and the pragmatics of their use (e.g., jargonistic uses of English and grammatical and syntactical differences between languages). In addition, signed language interpreting is frequently performed on a one-to-one basis, making the work highly labor-intensive. Demand for interpreting services in Australia currently outweighs the supply of accredited practitioners, which might lead one to expect that premium fees would be paid to interpreters in the field. However, while high fees are charged by many interpreting agencies for the services provided, monetary rewards do not always flow on to individual interpreters. Administration costs are normally cited as the culprit in reducing the wage paid to the interpreter.

Even though there has been an enormous increase in women's participation in the work force, the increase has occurred in those occupations, industries, and forms of employment in which women have always been overrepresented, such as service industries. This has not automatically given women enhanced leverage as workers. For example, in the area of pay levels, women continue to lag behind men. This difference is partly because many women work part-time, and the female work force is younger than the male.

Even if just the average weekly earnings of full-time-working adult men and women are compared, women still earn less than men (Probert, 1990, p. 101). The Australian Bureau of Statistics (ABS) reports that, as of May 1998, full-time adult nonmanagerial males earned $792.50 compared with $657.80 for females (ABS, 1998, p. 3). When all categories of employees are combined, the gap is even larger. The same ABS report indicates that males had higher average weekly total earnings than females—$729.20 compared with $483.10. The difference is reversed when part-time employees are compared: In 1998, the average weekly total earnings for male part-time employees was $265.50 compared with $284.50 for females (ABS, 1998, p. 3).

The marginalization of certain sectors of the labor market is significant because it has been recognized that there are gendered and ethnocentric constructions of injury and disease among different occupations and industries (Quinlan, 1992, p. 2; Williams & Thorpe, 1992, p. 153). As a result, hazards can be overlooked and injuries and illnesses underreported. Official statistics for women workers are lower than the actual rates of injury, and this is compounded by a tendency for women to underreport (Williams & Thorpe, 1992, p. 153).

In addition, the emphasis of workers' compensation has been on traumatic one-off injuries (such as fatalities, crushing, and amputations), which mostly occur in men's work. This means that those injuries that are less visible and associated with typically *female* occupations (such as OOS injuries associated with light manufacturing, office work, and signed language interpreting; infections and back injuries associated with nursing; and the stress risks involved in service work) may be deemphasized or obscured. As will become clear later in this chapter, some of the interpreters interviewed for this study tended not to report injuries, either because of overt threats or because of prior experiences with management.

Women are in positions of low bargaining power and/or are marginalized in the consultative process; therefore the capacity to secure equal employment opportunity gains is reduced (Boreham et al., 1996, p. 53). In addition, attitudinal factors are also important. Boreham et al. (1996) assert that women are typically socialized to be "accepting, accommodating, and pleasant" and are frequently in work situations where loyalty to the employer tends to be assumed. Since women's poor position in the labor market is frequently the result of gender segmentation into low-paid, part-time work, Bennett (1994, p. 216) feels that it cannot be overcome by teaching women negotiation skills or by encouraging them to have confidence in their abilities. Rather, such counseling is hypocritical as it pastes a respectable veneer over structural problems.

It seems clear that any examination of the paid labor of women is inextricably linked to the unpaid work they do, which stems from caring for a family. A detailed examination of caring work and its implications for individuals constitutes the next section of this chapter.

CARING WORK

Caring is a basic human emotion. In general, states Graham (1991, p. 15), caring relationships are those involving women: It is usually the presence of a woman—as wife, mother, daughter, neighbor, friend—which marks out a relationship as potentially, at least, a caring one. Male relationships, by contrast, are seen to be mediated in a different way, with the bonds—ostensibly at least—based not upon compassion, but on competition.

The unique factor in caring work (such as teaching, nursing, social work, and interpreting (sometimes classified as *human services* work) is that its delivery requires knowledgeable and disciplined use of the worker's self to create a publicly observable facial and bodily display (Wharton, 1993, p. 206; Brill, 1990). Both family and professional commitments incorporate the notion that the needs, demands, and difficulties of other people should be women's major, if not exclusive, concern and that meeting these must take precedence over all other claims (Adams, 1971, pp. 558–559). In doing so, the worker must also manage his or her own emotions and, on occasion, publicly display an emotion that he or she may not necessarily privately feel (Wharton, 1993, p. 208).

Many signed language interpreters reported that they derive a feeling of satisfaction from their work in helping two parties communicate. Interpreters in this study made comments such as "meeting people's needs," "bridging a communication gap," and "facilitating communication" to describe positive features of their work. Connotations of caring are evident in all these comments. Also evident in the responses of subjects in this study was the overwhelming concern for the needs of others—notably the Deaf person—often to the detriment of the interpreter's health. This point is of central importance to this study and will be examined in following sections.

The work of signed language interpreters has many caring aspects. Interpreters are required to adhere to a code of ethics that encompasses confidentiality, accuracy, impartiality, and professional distance. Like other caring workers, signed language interpreters may feel some tension between their adherence to this code and their genuine desire to help the individuals with whom they work. It is argued that the objective of remaining neutral and impartial is made more difficult because the historical role of an interpreter was as a helper or advocate. In the past, the feeling of concern for a client by an interpreter was usually manifested in taking charge and doing for; whereas interpreters today strive to demonstrate this care and concern by working in an "impartial and professionally distant way as a conduit or facilitator of communication between two parties who do not speak the same language." The current philosophy of interpreters is to work with consumers, to facilitate greater empowerment for that person, rather than do for them. Thus, there may be a tension between personal and professional norms of caring behavior.

Implications of Caring Work for Employment Opportunity

Graham (1991, p. 16) states that caring tends to be associated not only with women, but with those places where intimate relations with women are found. Specifically, caring is associated with the home and family. By contrast, relationships contracted within the labor market contain a degree of social distance incompatible with the giving of care. There are exceptions, of course—occupations where the woman's touch has been formally incorporated into the job specification. These occupations, interestingly, have a special designation: They are the caring professions in which the work force is largely female. In social work, secretarial work, retail sales, production of food, and preschool and primary school teaching, social relations are mediated through care with:

> the synthesising function traditionally discharged by women . . . translated to a wider sphere beyond the home. Instead of (or in addition to) keeping the family intact and maximally functional, women become involved in house-keeping tasks on behalf of society at large (Adams, 1971, p. 558).

Statham, Muller, and Mauksch (1988) state that many tasks in traditionally female occupations are considered natural for women—an extension of their gender role—and these are not classified as skilled work, and often are not classified as work at all. If women perform certain work naturally with no special training or skill, then the argument can be made that women's work could conceivably be handled by any female and does not require high levels of remuneration. Given that signed language interpreting has grown out of the welfare/counseling arena, the occupation may be viewed as an appropriate choice for women because the caring connotations attributed to this type of work fit with the cultural view of women as carers and nurturers. Caring and communication are often seen as natural for women, hence not part of a job, and certainly not something to be well rewarded financially.

Service work is an unending, unspecific task of helping, nurturing, educating, and supporting (Finch & Groves, 1983, p. 27). The persistent and continual nature of caring work can be highlighted thus: "Caring is experienced as a labour of love in which the labour must continue even where the love falters" (Finch & Groves, 1983, p. 16). This definition suggests that caring demands both love and labor, both identity and activity, with the nature of demands being shaped by the social interactions of the wider society. In gender-divided societies like ours, caring tends to have particular consequences for the identity and activity of women (Graham, 1991, p. 13).

A great many signed language interpreters interviewed for this study reported that their work was demanding and did, at times, seem monotonous and unending. Some commented on the almost never-ending stream of assignments they faced in a day and the strain of driving (sometimes long distances) from one appointment to the next. Others expressed frustration and fatigue at repeatedly encountering the same negative issues at each location before the interpreting work could commence. These issues include establishing the method of communication with the Deaf consumer, clarifying the interpreter's role, educating the consumers in the use of the interpreter, and negotiating the position from which the interpreter will work—all within a very short time frame. Many of the interpreters in this study stated that they felt that much more education of consumers was required.

There appears to be a conflict for many interpreters between performance of the job, the motivation for doing the job, and the financial aspects of the job (the value of the work). For many of the interpreters interviewed, the dominance of caring over the self is the norm, which in turn creates a great deal of stress for the interpreter. For example,

A couple of weeks ago I'd gone for about fifty minutes and I said to the client, "Look I'm going to have to stop now," and he said, "You can't stop now." I said, "I have to stop now." "Look," I said, "I'm getting really tired. I'm making mistakes, and I know I'll make a mistake." And he said, "That doesn't matter. Just keep going; we're nearly finished." So I did and I really felt drained at the end. I think I ended up going for an hour and a quarter. I know a lot of people go for a lot longer than that, but I can feel myself getting tired and I can feel myself making mistakes. I think that often different clients need to be aware of the interpreters. I don't think that, well, they can't have any concept of what it's like to be an interpreter, the same way you can't have any concept of what it's like to be Deaf, and I guess that that's a negative—they don't understand. We just try and keep going. You're sort of thinking of the client and you've got to think of yourself. I don't think it happens very often. (I 140, female signed language interpreter, employed on a freelance basis)

The comments made by interpreters interviewed for this study show that while the idealism to be superhuman is common, the conditions of their labor process undermine their professionalism and their OHS status.

The strong caring nature of signed language interpreters is captured in the following comments made by two of the interpreters in this study:

I just don't like feeling guilty because there are times when I just have to say no, but at the same time I'm always thinking, "Try [to get] somebody else. If you can't get anybody else, then get back to me". . . . The thought of the deaf person being there without anyone to facilitate the information really worries me, and sometimes things can't be put off, but I'm getting better at saying "no." It's still the thought of not being attended to in that sense, but sometimes it's a real emergency and it needs to be serviced. (I 41, female signed language interpreter, employed on a part-time freelance basis)

We try to do every job we can, but sometimes you just can't meet the demand. I just have to say no and be firm and not feel guilty. I used to feel guilty when I couldn't do a job. (I 50 , female signed language interpreter, employed on a full-time basis)

Signed language interpreters have traditionally worked alone during each of their assignments, in situations where none of the parties with whom they work have any real idea of what it is that the interpreter does. At present, while some employers send two interpreters to lengthy interpreting assignments, it is not uncommon for a freelance interpreter to work for several days, or perhaps a week, without the opportunity to converse with a colleague. This makes debriefing, support, recognition, and discussion of personal needs difficult, and may exacerbate the interpreter's feelings of isolation. It additionally creates serious health and safety concerns because of the potential for intensification of work.

In this potentially isolating employment situation, signed language interpreters tend to give up on recognition of their self (in fact, many strive to be invisible and seek to be ignored as participants in the situation). Interpreters function, by their own definition, as conduits or facilitators of communication only—who do not take part in or attempt to influence the situation. This overwhelming orientation to their work and clients leads to the tendency to deny the validity of their own needs, particularly with regard to their health and safety.

> The migraines come from not feeling comfortable about doing an assignment, really getting quite worked up. That has happened for rape cases. I remember one of them went continuously. The victim was in the witness box for four consecutive days. Now I thought I was the person raped in the end because you put yourself in the first person all the time. The interrogation and the cross-examining you know. . . . She was crying and crying and crying and giving that voice projection across too. You've got the jury sitting there and you can see the men going, "Oh, come on." [It was] just awful. My body kept going and when we had finished, I was history for two days. I was out of it and had to have injections to stop the vomiting. (I 42, female signed language interpreter, employed on a part-time basis)

The disastrous consequences of caring for the participants to the detriment of one's own needs are clearly demonstrated in the above quote. This interpreter, whilst in the role of a facilitator of communication between the rape victim and the court, found herself identifying strongly with the victim. Given that the interpreter was voicing not only the content of the victim's message, but also the tone and emotion that she was expressing, it is not hard to imagine that the interpreter would take on the persona of the woman giving evidence and empathize with the feelings being expressed. The net result for the interpreter, however, was that at the end of the interpreting assignment, her physical health was severely damaged. The long-term consequences of repeated experiences such as this are of great concern for the occupational health and safety of signed language interpreters.

In sum, the predominantly part-time and insecure nature of the job of an interpreter, the lack of institutional support and educational barriers to entry, the preponderance of women in the job, the struggle for professional status, the physical and mental tasks involved in the job tasks, and the volume of work for which interpreters are required all create enormous pressures on signed language interpreters. Consequently, interpreters do not yet enjoy professional status in any aspects of their work. Some individuals develop effective coping strategies to control the conditions of their work and deal with the pressures, while others withdraw from the labor market, develop restrictive labor practices (such as taking on less work) in order to cope, and many fall victim to work-related illness or injury. One injury that flows directly from the structural pressures in the employment of signed language interpreters epitomizes their lack of control over the tasks and conditions of work: OOS, which was previously known as Repetitive Strain Injury (RSI). The following section focuses on a definition of OOS and casual factors relating to the occurrence of these injuries.

OCCUPATIONAL OVERUSE SYNDROME

Definition

The National Occupational Health and Safety Commission (NOHSC) defines Occupational Overuse Syndrome (OOS) as

> A collective term for a range of conditions characterised by discomfort or persistent pain in muscles, tendons and other soft tissues, with or without physical manifestations ... [Occupational Overuse Syndrome] is usually caused or aggravated by work and is associated with repetitive movement, sustained or constrained postures and/or forceful movements (NOHSC, quoted in Ewan et al., 1991, p. 169).

OOS was previously known as Repetitive (or Repetition) Strain Injury (RSI). Hopkins (1989, p. 251) noted that *RSI* is not medically precise, being used more as an "umbrella" term, and rarely appears in official statistics on work-related injury.

McDermott (1989, p. 197) states that the clinical features of OOS include pain, tenderness, weakness, swelling, numbness or paraesthesia. Pain occurs in all cases, and tenderness is usually evident.

Aetiology

OOS may result from tasks that impose a static load on the postural muscles of the neck and shoulder region (such as raising the arms), as well as those involving static (low-repetition) and dynamic (high-repetition) loads on the arm and hand muscles (Rempel et al., 1992, p. 838; Moore et al., 1991, p. 1434; Maeda, quoted in McDermott, 1989, p. 198; Browne, Nolan & Faithfull, 1987). Other factors that are important in the development of OOS are generalized muscle load in uncomfortable working positions, mental stress or tension, unfavorable environmental factors, and poorly designed working conditions (Maeda, quoted in McDermott, 1989, p. 198).

Occupational overuse symptoms, whatever their cause, can be clinically divided into the following three stages, according to reversibility and outcome:

Stage 1. Aching and/or fatigue of affected limbs, which occurs during work shift, but settles overnight and on days off. There is no significant reduction of work performance and usually no physical signs, such as those which appear in later stages, for example, swelling or crepitus (crackling sensations). Usual signs may include muscle and tendon tenderness, fatigue, and discomfort. This condition can persist for weeks or months.

Stage 2. Recurrent aching and fatigue which increasingly occur earlier in the work shift and persist longer. Symptoms fail to settle overnight, cause sleep disturbance, and are associated with a reduced capacity for repetitive work. Physical signs such as swelling may be present. Tingling and burning sensations, pain and weakness, or loss of grip strength may also be present. This condition usually persists for months.

Stage 3. Persistent aching that prevents the use of any of the muscle group; fatigue and weakness at rest and pain occurs with nonrepetitive movements. The symptoms cause sleep disturbance. The person is unable to perform less-arduous or light duties and experiences difficulty with nonoccupational tasks. Physical signs such as swelling, numbness, color or temperature changes, and crepitus are present. The condition may last for months or years (Browne et al., 1987).

OOS has been well-recognized as a serious health issue for many types of workers for decades. Among these are individuals engaged in process work in the electronics, white goods, electrical, automobile, and packaging industries (Ewan et al., 1991; Meekosha & Jakubowicz, 1986); keyboard or cash register operation (Bammer & Blignault, 1988; Mullaly & Grigg, 1988); musicians (Fry, 1986); and other forms of manual labor such as piece workers and outworkers in the clothing industry (Stevenson, 1988; Meekosha & Jakubowicz, 1986). However, only recently has the issue of OOS for signed language interpreters received attention (DeCaro, Feuerstein & Hurwitz, 1992; Feuerstein & Fitzgerald, 1992; Cergol, 1991; Cohn, Lowry, & Hart, 1990; Stedt, 1989; Meals, Payne & Gaines, 1988; Sanderson, 1987).

In examining the nature and extent of the so-called OOS "epidemic" in Australia, Bammer (1990, p. 23) found "little evidence for personal causes but strong evidence for work-related factors, particularly high pressure jobs where autonomy, variety and peer cohesion are lacking." Signed language interpreting fits the definition of a high-pressure job, largely owing to factors such as lack of control over working conditions, lack of peer cohesion, inconsistency in client expectations, and high volume of work.

The task of signed language interpretation is composed of a set of repetitive, forceful movements in conjunction with sometimes awkward postures of the fingers, hand, wrist, forearm, and shoulder—factors which have been outlined above as associated with the development of overuse injuries. The velocity and acceleration of finger and hand movements during signed language interpreting are quite high. The interpreting task also involves high static load on the muscles of the back, shoulders, neck, and upper arms.

Pain can result for signed language interpreters as a result of maintaining such abnormal positions for long periods. Interpreters traditionally have been trained to produce signs with the wrists flexed backwards and the forearms twisted outwards and kept straight to make the hands more clearly visible. This forced and limited range of movement clearly puts large amounts of abnormal stress on articular and soft tissue structures (Cohn et al., 1990, p. 209) and has the capacity to cause significant damage. One of the interpreters interviewed for this study described the task and its consequences for her in the following way:

> When I was interpreting, day after day, you are continually being bombarded with stimuli—the visual, or the auditory, everything. When you

get more and more tired and more fatigued, more stress, more adrenalin pumping, you begin to get to the stage where you go on automatic pilot. So that in the brain on a neurological level, your brain figured out the quickest pathways from point A to point B, which is where to want to get every day, and it takes it on automatic pilot. When I got more and more tired . . . it short-circuited and it started taking different paths, and the paths it took was the pain. So that every time I would start to interpret, I would feel the pain, and then it got to the stage that every time I would used my hands I would feel the pain. . . . I had to basically learn to do everything again. I learned to walk again. I learned to move my jaw again. I learned to speak. I learned to use my eyes again. At the moment I'm learning to use my fingers again. (I 136, female signed language interpreter, employed on a part-time basis, has a diagnosed OOS condition)

Occupational overuse is a hazard for signed language interpreters particularly when interpreting in classroom and public speaking situations. In these physically and mentally demanding situations, the interpreter must produce clear signs, often in a large space in front of the body, and must keep pace with the presenter (no matter how fast he or she may be speaking). The process of interpreting in these types of "machine-paced" situations is very demanding. In voice-to-sign interpreting, the interpreter must listen to the speaker, understand what is being said, then choose and produce the appropriate signs and correct grammatical order to convey the message to the Deaf person. Many speakers tend to talk very quickly, and when the interpreter lags behind the speaker by one or two sentences, it means that he or she is listening and processing new information while signing a previous message—which is extremely stressful.

Studies into the prevalence of overuse injuries among signed language interpreters in American educational institutions report rates of between 18% (Cohn et al., 1990) and 59–60% (DeCaro et al., 1992; Feuerstein & Fitzgerald, 1992), indicating that the problem is a significant one for these workers.

Effects of OOS

Bammer and Blignault (1988) report that people suffering from OOS have difficulty performing a variety of activities of daily living, including using a telephone, writing, attending to personal hygiene, dressing, manipulating cutlery, vacuuming, and driving. Sanderson (1987) also notes that the non-physical symptoms are even more disturbing than the physical sensations experienced by OOS sufferers. People begin to feel clumsy; small tasks like brushing one's teeth or picking up a coffee cup become difficult or painful.

In addition to these physical difficulties, sufferers may also display symptoms of worry, tension, bewilderment, depression, guilt, feelings of hopelessness and helplessness, inferiority, stigmatization, fear, and anger. Bammer and Blignault (1988) note anecdotal evidence which suggests that marital and family difficulties, even breakdown and withdrawal from social activities, are common consequences of OOS. Similar effects from OOS were documented in Ewan et al. (1991):

> [the feeling of] loss of control over lives, [having] an invisible disability, loss of paid work, loss of income . . . [difficulties with] the compensation system, difficulties with household tasks and self-care and tensions with families (Ewan et al., 1991:176).

Additionally, many routine activities of life, ranging from simple social engagements to returning to work, become problematic and uncertain because sufferers can not predict the course of events in any given day, month, or even year (Ewan et al., 1991, p. 176).

> It has certainly affected parts of my life. I can't go canoeing or bungy jumping, lots of things like that I've always wanted to do in my life, I probably won't be able to do them. Lots and lots of things like that have affected my life. I don't run. I don't play netball. I don't do any sport. I'm very unfit, so all that side of my life has been affected. When I go to a party or something, it's just not the same. My life is not the same. I used to be a real never-sit-still type of person, now I'm just a blob. That's the shocking side: I just can't take myself into the city—I just can't do it. (I 144, female signed language interpreter, not working, has a diagnosed OOS condition)

Meekhosha and Jakubowicz (1986, p. 398) also note that a further result of losing one's job following the development of OOS and "going back into the home" is depression. Depression is more than just a consequence of the physical pain, or the loss of a job, or the inability to use one's limbs. It has also been termed the "loss of self"—the undermining experience of living a restricted life, being socially isolated, experiencing discredited definitions of self, and becoming a burden to others (Charmaz, 1983, p. 34).

A major reason for the loss of self is that not only is the injured woman suddenly unproductive in the public sphere of work, and thus literally without value, but she is even unable to fulfil tasks expected of a mother and housewife. The experience of "becoming nothing" is evident in the loss of identity as independent working women and as vital family members. For many injured women, the identity as a worker is a valued one, which confers above all financial security, but also independence and a sense of achievement in successfully combining the roles of home manager, mother, and worker (Ewan et al., 1991, p. 185). Bammer and Blignault (1988, p. 392) report that people with overuse injuries go through a process analogous to grieving, having to negotiate shock, denial, sadness, anger, guilt, and depression before reaching the stage of acceptance necessary for coping with their new situation.

Stresses for signed language interpreters are best summed up by James DeCaro, former Dean, National Technical Institute for the Deaf, Rochester, New York:

> Interpreting is much more than an occupation—it's a lifestyle and a culture. People become interpreters because they care about working in the Deaf community and when they become injured, they are deprived of an opportunity to interact with people whom they've grown to know and respect (Cergol, 1991, p. 16).

STATEMENT OF HYPOTHESES

It was therefore hypothesized that because signed language interpreters are at high risk of suffering from work processes and conditions which are intense and demanding for long periods, these workers would be at risk of developing OOS. Therefore, one of the aims of this study was to identify a number of factors which may be associated with the development of OOS among signed language interpreters, including:

1. the gender of the population affected;
2. the length of time individuals had worked as interpreters (those who have worked for a greater number of years may be worse affected);
3. work status (those who worked part-time or on a freelance basis may have been worse affected because of work pressures and job insecurity); and

4. job duration (those who worked for longer periods at a time may have been worse affected than those who worked shorter periods).

All of the above factors may, or may not, have operated individually or in combination. It was also hypothesized that the individual's experience with OOS would have a negative influence on aspects of that individual's personal, social, and family life, and ultimately that individual's desire to stay in the occupation.

DESIGN, PROCEDURE, AND SUBJECTS

OOS represents a complex variety of symptoms and conditions for which medical personnel have found difficulty in identifying specific causes. As such, experimental approaches which serve to measure the frequency of conditions or the differential effects of two or more syndromes upon the signed language interpreter's ability to continue to work were inappropriate for this study.

Hence, it was believed that the use of individual questionnaires with quantitative and qualitative data and follow-up in-depth interviews would yield data most useful in testing the hypotheses and achieving the aims of this project. An evaluation of the work environment from the worker's own point of view was of interest since assessment of the subjective as well as objective well-being of the worker was one goal of this research.

The following types of data were of interest in this study:

1. descriptions of level, duration, and frequency of exposure to different interpreting loads in the work environment;
2. descriptions of the response to a certain environmental load (which can include physical and psychological repercussions);
3. descriptions of specific physiological effects from work, which can be linked to OOS; and
4. descriptions of individual characteristics which might affect one's response to the work environment and ability to cope with the injury (e.g., home task demands, hobbies).

Specific information on all of the above factors (with the possible exception of factor 1) is not readily gathered through the use of quantitative methods. Hence the completion of a follow-up interview with each questionnaire respondent was planned to obtain more personalized data. (The content of the questionnaire and procedure for distribution is explained below.)

Procedure

The aim of this study was to make as comprehensive a survey as possible of all signed language interpreters in Australia. At the time the survey was undertaken, the total number of signed language interpreters in each state in Australia was small (national total 165). A list of potential subjects for the study was generated from signed language interpreters registered in the 1991 edition of the *NAATI Directory* and from the membership records of state and territory branches of ASLIA. All individuals discovered from these two key sources were sent a copy of a 44-item anonymous response questionnaire with a cover letter explaining the purposes of the study. The questionnaire items were designed to provide objective quantitative data. In addition, a few open-ended questions on more subjective topics (such as positive and negative aspects of the job, level of support received, and job satisfaction in general) were included.

Specifically, the questionnaire (adapted from Shadbolt, 1988) was designed to gather information about:

1. Respondents' age, sex, first language, educational level attained, as well as a number of aspects of their working lives, such as length of time in the profession, current work status (e.g., part-time or full-time), level of accreditation, and work history (the information on accreditation levels of the subject pool is displayed in Table 1. Table 2 shows age and gender characteristics). Information was also sought about the length of time subjects had suffered from an OOS, the number of times they had been off work on medical advice because of OOS, and whether or not the symptoms of OOS had been alleviated.
2. The extent to which situations or conditions that are potentially stressful were present in subjects' lives.
3. The degree of psychosocial stress subjects experienced from interactions with workmates and changes in career aspirations were assessed.
4. The severity of life strains being experienced by subjects was assessed.

5. Job satisfaction was measured by four separate single item variables.

After the date for the return of the questionnaire had passed, those who had not responded were contacted by telephone in order to determine their willingness to be involved in the research. Any individuals interested in inclusion were granted an additional week to return the questionnaire. The names of those not interested were removed from records, and they were not contacted again (n = 46). A total of 106 questionnaires were returned (64%). This was considered to be an excellent response rate, indicative of interpreters' interest in the topic.

The respondent pool was made up of 81 women and 25 men. All subjects except two regularly performed interpreting work. Questionnaire respondents came from all states and territories in Australia, with the exception of the Northern Territory. A description of the subjects' characteristics appears in the tables and figures below.

After the final questionnaire return date, a schedule of interviews for all respondents was drawn up. All interviews were conducted on an individual face-to-face basis in the capital city of the subject's home state. The interviews (consisting of 66 questions and lasting an average of 90 minutes) were conducted in a private room on the local Deaf Society premises. A total of 93 interviews were conducted and recorded on audiotape (with the subject's permission) and later transcribed. (Interviews were not conducted with respondents in the Australian Capital Territory and Tasmania due to logistical difficulties in visiting these two areas, n = 7.) Also, a number of interpreters who had returned a questionnaire were not able to attend an interview (n = 6).

The interview was designed to expand upon responses to questionnaire items. Respondents were also encouraged to provide detailed subjective information in regard to their feelings about any pain suffered and its effects. A number of additional attitudinal issues (such as level of perceived support from fellow workers, spouses, and supervisors; evaluation of job and work tasks; and opinions of societal perception of job) were raised in the interview.

Weakness in Research Design

A potential threat to the validity of using subjective interviewee evaluations in the interview was that the subjects may have allowed their ideology rather than their personal experience to influence responses. Other possible problems might have been those of response bias; that is, those most interested and/or affected by OOS may have been the most likely to respond. In order to avoid such bias, the author interviewed all respondents, rather than only those who suffered from OOS.

Second, the interviewees may have avoided extreme response alternatives. Third, given that the subjects are a caring group of workers, social desirability, striving to give a positive impression, and having a tendency to consider clients before self may have diminished the number of negative responses. A problem related to this last point is that, in some cases, the subjects may have had reason to believe that their answers may have important consequences for themselves. Hence they may have underreported injuries if their job security was threatened or they were under enforced change of job, lacked economic compensation, or had insufficient sick leave. These possibilities could obviously have influenced their answers. These possibilities were compensated for by the inclusion of a number of items to check the respondents' consistency. In addition, a guarantee of total confidentiality of all identifiable data was given, and no identifying information was included on the record of interviews.

Response Rates and Accreditation Level of Subjects

Table 1 shows the number of subjects who returned a completed questionnaire and were included in this study. The number in the "not included" column indicates those who did not return the questionnaire and whose names were removed from records. The table also shows details of the subjects' accreditation level.

The majority of subjects in this thesis were accredited at level 2 (now known as paraprofessional interpreter accreditation) (60% of the total). However, a higher return rate was achieved from those subjects accredited at level 3 (now known as interpreter accreditation) (88% for interpreters as compared with 76% for paraprofessional interpreters). This variation in response rates may be due to the fact that level 3 interpreters have generally been in the field longer and may be more highly motivated to maintain contact via the NAATI directory and by listing a current

TABLE 1. *Subjects' NAATI Interpreting Accreditation Level*

Accreditation Level	Included	Not Included	Total
Language Aide (Level 1)	8 (66%)	4 (34%)	12 (9%)
Paraprofessional			
Interpreter (Level 2)	62 (76%)	19 (23%)	81 (60%)
Interpreter (Level 3)	29 (88%)	4 (12%)	32 (24%)
No accreditation	7 (77%)	2 (22%)	9 (7%)
Total	106	29	135

Note. Numbers in parentheses indicate percentage of total population for that level.

address. They may also, as more highly qualified interpreters, have a greater interest in research projects into their developing profession and be more willing to participate. This study may have been perceived as assisting in the professionalization of the occupation.

Age and Gender Distribution of Subjects

A characteristic of general interest to the study was the age range of individuals and the proportion of females and males in the subject pool. Table 2 shows the age and gender characteristics of subjects. The number of subjects in each 10-year age category (from less than 20 years of age to over 60 years of age) is shown, as well as the number of males and females in each age category.

The sample was more heavily populated by women (76%). The age range for both female and male interpreters covers almost the entire range measured (i.e., from less than 20 to 59 years of age).

Employment Status of Subjects

The basis upon which subjects were employed is shown in Table 3.

The majority of subjects (59%) worked on a part-time (generally this was permanent part-time work or a consistent number of hours worked each week) or casual basis (meaning a varying number of hours worked each week). This part-time category includes those interpreters who reported they worked on a freelance basis. The majority of part-time or casual positions were held by women (87% of part-

TABLE 2. *Age and Gender Characteristics of Questionnaire Respondents*

Age	Female	Male	Total
<20 years	1 (50%)	1 (50%)	2 (2%)
20 – 29 years	22 (75%)	7 (25%)	29 (27%)
30 – 39 years	32 (80%)	8 (20%)	40 (37%)
40 – 49 years	23 (77%)	7 (23%)	30 (27%)
50 – 59 years	3 (75%)	1 (25%)	4 (4%)
> 60 years	0	1 (100%)	1 (1%)
Total	81 (76%)	25 (24%)	106

Note. Figures in parentheses indicate the percentage of the subjects in each age group.

TABLE 3. *Subjects' Current Employment Status*

	Full-time	Part-time	Casual	Not working	No response
Female	22 (55%)	33 (87%)	20 (95%)	2 (100%)	3 (60%)
Male	18 (45%)	5 (13%)	1 (5%)	0	2 (40%)
Total	40 (38%)	38 (36%)	21 (20%)	2 (2%)	5 (5%)

Note. Figures in parentheses indicate the percentage of the subjects in each employment group.

time jobs and 95% of casual or freelance jobs). Just over one-third of the subjects (38%) held a full-time position.

Types of casual or part-time work included educational interpreting in secondary schools or universities, freelance community interpreting through an interpreting agency, or freelance work as a result of direct personal approaches. These data suggest that most work for signed language interpreters is on a part-time basis.

First Language Status of Subjects

Twenty-seven of the subjects (25%) identified Auslan as their first language, that is, they grew up in a family where Auslan was predominantly used (their parents were Deaf). Of the remaining 79 respondents (75%), 73 (69%) indicated that Auslan was not their first language. Six respondents did not answer the question. No data were collected as to whether a language other than English was spoken by any of the respondents.

Family Status of Subjects

Sixty percent of questionnaire respondents were married ($n = 65$; 50 women and 15 men). Of the remainder, 20% were single ($n = 21$; 13 women and 8 men), 2% were separated ($n = 2$ women), 8% were divorced ($n = 8$ women), 4% were in a de facto relationship ($n = 4$; 3 women and 1 man), and 6% did not reply to this question ($n = 6$; 5 women and 1 man).

Prevalence of Medically Diagnosed OOS

Twenty-three (22%) of the 106 subjects (5 male, 18 female) reported a medically diagnosed OOS in the questionnaire responses. Conditions diagnosed included carpal tunnel syndrome (two cases), ulnar nerve entrapment, epicondylitis (three cases), "elbow and wrist pain," "shoulder and neck strain," "upper arm pain," and "sore arms" (one of each). However, only 10 of these 23 subjects, (nine females, one male) (44%) reported that they had taken time off work on medical advice. Time away from work varied from one day (recovery from a cortisone injection) to two-and-a-half years. Only 6 of these 23 respondents (26%) reported that the injury had been resolved.

Of the 13 individuals suffering from a diagnosed OOS who did not take time off work, only four (three females, one male) (29%) reported that the injury symptoms had been alleviated. The reasons given for not taking time off work included:

- Treatment and advice from chiropractor was sufficient. (I 83, female signed language interpreter, employed on a full-time basis, OOS condition resolved);
- Not serious enough—and after learning to relax more while working, the problem dissipated. (I 55, female signed language interpreter, employed on a part-time basis, OOS condition resolved);
- High demand for services—eventually I would have to catch up anyway. (I 19, male signed language interpreter, employed on a full-time basis, OOS condition unresolved);
- Could not afford to [take time off], as I was freelance at the time. Worked with terribly painful arms and hands. (I 79, female signed language interpreter, employed on a full-time basis, OOS condition unresolved);

- I ignored medical advice because the injury took too long to heal (six months). It was difficult to find a replacement. I was enjoying my job. (I 96, male signed language interpreter, employed on a full-time basis, OOS condition unresolved); and
- Because of freelance [work], just didn't ask for work. Chose only short jobs or shared jobs. (I 105, female signed language interpreter, employed on a casual basis, OOS condition unresolved)

It is disturbing that eight of these 13 subjects (62%) did not take time off work and continued to work with their pain not alleviated to any great extent. In addition, another 11 respondents (10%) reported symptoms indicative of OOS, for which no diagnosis, treatment, or adaptation of work procedures had occurred or even been sought. This means that a total of 34 subjects of the 106 interpreters who returned a questionnaire (32%) were significantly affected in terms of their work health.

Prevalence of Symptoms of OOS

In addition to the effect that OOS-related injury had on work performance, it was hypothesized that some subjects would experience discomfort and/or difficulty in performing everyday tasks. Table 4 shows data relating to the level of difficulty experienced by subjects in performing a given number of everyday household tasks. The column headed "OOS" shows responses from subjects who have been diagnosed as suffering from OOS. (Note: the heading "No OOS" refers only to lack of medical diagnosis: There may be some OOS cases in this category.)

These data indicate that a significant proportion of the subjects who did not report a medically diagnosed OOS nonetheless experienced varying degrees of difficulty in undertaking some everyday tasks, particularly brushing their hair, cutting up food, writing, and pegging out washing (all of which are symptomatic of an OOS condition). One might therefore suspect that the prevalence of OOS among signed language interpreters is somewhat higher than has been diagnosed (or even recognized).

It may be considered that more women than men would suffer from OOS, because slighter musculature might make them more susceptible. A 2 x 2 contingency table of gender and prevalence of OOS was therefore generated as follows for chi square analysis (Table 5).

TABLE 4. *Subjects' Self-Reported Level of Difficulty Performing Everyday Tasks*

Task	No difficulty		Little difficulty		Great difficulty		Unable to perform	
	OOS	No OOS	OOS	No OOS	OOS	No OOS	OOS	No OOS
Cut nails	16 (73%)	76	3 (14%)	0	1 (5%)	0	2 (9%)	0
Cut food	15 (68%)	75	3 (14%)	3	2 (9%)	0	1 (5%)	0
Brush hair	16 (68%)	72	3 (14%)	4	2 (9%)	0	1 (5%)	0
Brush teeth	16 (68%)	76	4 (18%)	0	1 (5%)	0	1 (5%)	0
Write (letters)	8 (36%)	68	9 (40%)	8	4 (18%)	0	1 (5%)	0
Shower/ bathe	18 (81%)	76	1 (5%)	0	2 (9%)	0	1 (5%)	0
Dress self	16 (68%)	75	4 (18%)	1	1 (5%)	0	1 (5%)	0
Drive a car	10 (46%)	74	6 (27%)	1	4 (18%)	0	2 (9%)	0
Peg out washing	11 (50%)	71	6 (27%)	4	3 (14%)	1	2 (9%)	0

Note. Figures in parentheses represent the percentage of subjects in the "OOS.

Chi square analysis indicated that the relationship between gender and OOS was not significant (X^2 = 0.0555; df = 1; $p < 1$). No more women than men suffer from OOS.

Job Experience and Exposure

Length of employment as a signed language interpreter and level of exposure to risk of injury were considered important variables in the development of OOS. Table 6 shows the number of years subjects had spent in paid interpreting work. The total of respondents is only 100 as six subjects did not respond to this question.

The male population was polarized between those who were relatively new to the occupation (One-third having been employed for one to three years), and those who had been in the occupation for longer than seven years (50%). The work experience of the females was more varied than the male subjects, being spread out from one year to more than nine years.

Table 7 shows the prevalence of diagnosed OOS in the subject pool.

The prevalence of diagnosed OOS was lower for the less-experienced group (12% for those who had been in the field for up to three years)

TABLE 5. *Contingency Table of Gender and Prevalence of OOS*

	OOS	No OOS	Total
Male	5	20	25
Female	18	63	81
Total	25	83	106

than for those who had been engaged in employment for a longer period of time (68% for those in the field for more than seven years). This result from the analysis suggests that there may be some dose/response relationship. A 5 x 2 contingency table of prevalence of OOS and years employed as an interpreter was therefore generated for chi square analysis (Table 8).

Chi square analysis indicated that the relationship between years employed as an interpreter and presence of OOS was not significant (X^2 = 6.841; df = 4; $p < 0.20$). It therefore appears that it does not matter how long one works as an interpreter; one is likely to develop an OOS due to the nature and organization of the work, not merely from longer service. It appears that the nature of the physical demands of interpreting are such that any interpreter, no matter how long in the field, is susceptible to injury. Clearly, preventative strategies must be put in place to avoid injury for signed language interpreters.

Notably, the decline in incidence in the "greater than nine years" group indicates that the period of employment is not the only relevant factor. This result may also mean that interpreters who suffer from OOS are more likely than nonsufferers to leave the interpreting field. To further elucidate the dose/response relationship mentioned above, part- and full-time workers were compared.

Job Tenure

Table 9 shows the rate of diagnosed OOS for those in full-time and part-time employment (N.B., for this table, "part-time" includes casual and freelance employment categories).

As these data show, the greatest proportion of OOS occurred among full-time workers (27% as compared with 18% for part-time employees). A 2 x 2 contingency table of prevalence of OOS and employment status was generated for chi square analysis (Table 10).

TABLE 6. *Length of Time Questionnaire Respondents Have Spent in Paid Employment as an Interpreter*

No. of years	Female	Male	Total
< 1 year	7 (88%)	1 (12%)	8 (8%)
1-3 years	26 (79%)	7 (21%)	33 (33%)
4-6 years	20 (83%)	4 (17%)	24 (24%)
7-9 years	9 (90%)	1 (10%)	10 (10%)
> 9 years	14 (56%)	11 (44%)	25 (25%)
Total	76	24	100

Note. Figures in parentheses indicate the percentage of the total subjects in each category.

Chi square analysis indicated that the relationship between employment status and OOS was not significant (X^2 = 1.123; df = 1; $</p < 1$). There appears to be.no statistically significant link between work status and increased likelihood of OOS, although there is a trend apparent. Results indicate a relationship for all types of employees. Further, it may be that because of the development of an OOS condition, full-time workers changed their work duration to part-time, somewhat obscuring the analysis of this issue.

Work Duration

As OOS is a cumulative injury, it was considered important to examine the length of time per day the interpreters were engaged in interpreting work. Table 11 shows the interpreting work duration by hours worked per day.

The table shows that the highest prevalence of diagnosed OOS occurred among those who worked for the greatest period of uninterrupted time (i.e., a rate of 35% for those interpreters who worked more than four hours per day). A 5 x 2 contingency table of prevalence of OOS and work duration was generated for chi square analysis (Table 12).

Chi square analysis indicated that the relationship between work duration and OOS was not significant (X^2 = 2.541; df = 4; $p < 1$). It appears that even comparatively short durations of work (i.e., four hours per day) resulted in a similar incidence of OOS as longer durations.

TABLE 7. *Number of Years Subjects Have Spent in Interpreting;
OOS Versus No OOS Diagnosed*

	<1 year	1 – 3 years	4 – 6 years	7 – 9 years	> 9 years
OOS	0 (0%)	4 (12%)	6 (25%)	4 (40%)	7 (28%)
No OOS	8 (100%)	29 (88%)	18 (75%)	6 (60%)	18 (75%)

Note. Figures in parentheses indicate the percentage of the total individuals in each category.

Effect of Interpreting Work and OOS on Private Life

A limited exploration was conducted on the effects of interpreting work upon aspects of the subjects' everyday lives, namely personal relationships, family, and social life. Data have been separated for those with and without diagnosed OOS. Questionnaire responses are presented in Table 13.

For personal relationships, 38% of OOS subjects reported a "very strong" effect, while 25% reported a "strong" effect. (The effects, which could have been positive or negative, were explored during the follow-up interview.) Among the subjects who do not have a diagnosed OOS condition, 62% indicated a "very strong" effect, and 70% reported a "strong" effect. Interpreters who do not have a diagnosed OOS condition tended to indicate a more significant impact than those with OOS. This is the opposite of the expected result. The level and nature of effect was highlighted in responses during interviews:

> I think it's got a strong effect on my personal relationships like [with] my husband, because I really like my job. It's the first job I've had that I've felt fully satisfied. I think in the negative too, it has an effect, because my husband sees his job as not important. When we meet people and they say "What do you do?" he feels like after I've said what I do, that it's up on some high pedestal for some reason and his isn't, which I don't feel, but he feels. I think that it has a negative effect [on] that whole macho man image. (I 9, female signed language interpreter, employed on a casual basis, does not have a diagnosed OOS condition)

> I think we are in a double barrel situation because [my wife] is involved in a job which has similar sorts of demands to this one, and it goes back to the irregular hours and how that encroaches on your personal life…. It's not this sort of regular thing where you're home by

TABLE 8. *Contingency Table of Prevalence of OOS and Years Employed as an Interpreter*

	<1	1 – 3	4 – 6	7 – 9	> 9	Total
OOS	0	4	6	4	7	21
No OOS	8	29	18	6	18	79
Total	8	33	24	10	25	100

six and you get the dinner and you watch a bit of telly. That hardly ever happens, and that goes into the weekend [too]. The weekends where you actually have a full weekend at home are few and far between, and that affects your personal relationships. (I 43, male signed language interpreter, employed on a full-time basis, does not have a diagnosed OOS condition)

For family relationships, 35% of OOS subjects indicated that their interpreting work had a "very strong" effect. The percentage for "strong" effect reported by interpreters who have a diagnosed OOS condition is 22%. The percentages for the interpreters who do not have an OOS-related condition are 65% and 72%, respectively. That is, those who did not have a diagnosed OOS condition indicate more impact from work on their personal life, which again could have been perceived as negative or positive. Responses of "no effect" were 5% for the OOS group and 91% for the other subjects. During the interviews, interpreters responded to a follow-up question on this issue in the following ways:

For family life, I guess it affects because I come from a Deaf family and I work in the Deaf field. I think sometimes I feel like when I visit Mum and Dad, they come up with something they want me to give them some assistance on, I think, "Oh no, this is work again and I came for a family visit. Where did our family visit go?" That sort of wears down your level of tolerance of doing those sorts of things. (I 43, male signed language interpreter, employed on a full-time basis, does not have a diagnosed OOS condition)

My first marriage split up and I have a feeling that work had a lot to do with it. The fact that he didn't want me to work in the first place and when I did, it was quite a demanding job. . . . A lot of things you do end up doing is with Deaf people or you run into Deaf people. I feel as though with your social life, you can't do anything without running

TABLE 9. *Prevalence of OOS Related to Work Status*

Full-Time		Part-Time	
OOS	No OOS	OOS	No OOS
11 (27%)	30 (73%)	10 (18%)	46 (82%)

Note. Figures in parentheses represent the percentage of individuals for that category.

into them. My kids even eventually got to the point where they say, "Mum there's a Deaf person, quick let's run the other way"—because they know that I'll be there stuck talking for a while. I used to do a lot of socialising with the Deaf people. I used to go out with them a lot. Not so much now. (I 6, female signed language interpreter, employed on a part-time basis, does not have a diagnosed OOS condition)

For social relationships, 12% of OOS reported a "very strong" effect and 35% reported a "strong" effect. Eighty-two percent of non-OOS subjects reported "very strong" effect, while 59% of this group reported "strong" effect. For "no effect," the response rates were 10% and 90%, respectively. Some of the comments made during the interviews on the effect of interpreting work on social life were as follows:

The times do interfere with personal relationships, perhaps the things that you would like to do together, that you can't... I mean if you could sort of say, "Look, next Thursday night I'm not working." In a normal everyday job you could probably do that, but with interpreting it doesn't necessarily mean that you won't be working next Thursday. I mean 24 hours beforehand or even half an hour beforehand, your beeper could go off and you might have to go to work. . . . That has a strong effect. If you make a hairdressing appointment, I mean, my hair it just needs cutting quite badly, I just sort of say, "You know, on Friday I'm going to make an appointment to go to the hairdressers." Every time you make one, you have to cancel it, because there's a job that's come up or something. (I 137, female signed language interpreter, employed on a full-time basis, does not have a diagnosed OOS condition).

These percentages indicate that the job of interpreting has, overall, a profound ("strong" or "very strong") effect on all subjects in the areas of personal and family relationships (for the OOS subjects, the total percentages for these two categories are: 78% for personal relationships

TABLE 10. *Contingency Table of Prevalence of OOS and Employment Status*

	Part-time	Full-time	Total
OOS	10	11	21
No OOS	46	30	76
Total	56	41	97

and 74% for family relationships, as compared with 49% and 53%, respectively, for non-OOS subjects). The responses to "strong" or "very strong" effect on social life are 61% for those who have an OOS condition and 42% for the non-OOS subjects.

As mentioned above, the "very strong" or "strong" effects reported could be either positive or negative. Clarification was sought in follow-up interviews by asking the interviewees to explain why they had given their responses. Of particular interest was the relationship between marital satisfaction, OOS, and involvement in employment for women, as well as the potential conflict therein.

In the married subsample ($n = 28$ females and 7 males), only 17% of the females reported that their male partners took more responsibility for domestic duties than they did (as reported in the previous chapter). It is clear that the women in this study, though engaged in paid work on either a full- or part-time basis, are still far more likely to be involved in taking primary responsibility for most domestic labor and childcare. That is, as was discussed earlier, these caring women workers are at the cutting edge of dual allegiances.

OOS Experience and Career Aspirations

Of the 23 medically diagnosed OOS sufferers, 9 (39%) indicated that their career aspirations had not changed (although 1 commented that aspirations had "slowed"). Eleven (48%) indicated slight modification to career goals. Comments about career aspirations (made in writing on the questionnaire form) were as follows:

- Fear of RSI worsening, therefore unsure of what my aspirations for future should be. (I 2, female signed language interpreter, employed on a part-time basis);
- [I am] frightened I can't return to freelance full-time. I like mostly

TABLE 11. *Questionnaire Respondents' Work Duration (in Hours Per Day) Related to the Prevalence of OOS*

< 1 hour		1 – 2 hours		2 – 3 hours		3 – 4 hours		> 4 hours		not working	
OOS	No OOS	OOS	No OOS	OOS	No OOS	OOS	No OOS	OOS	No OOS	OOS	No OOS
2	8	1	10	3	16	4	12	4	8	8	24
(20%)		(9%)		(16%)		(25%)		(33%)		(25%)	

educational work which requires long hours of interpreting—alone. (I 79, female signed language interpreter, employed on a full-time basis); and

- [I] will not normally work alone; will not do full-time freelance; limit number of hours of interpreting work per week. (I 87, female signed language interpreter, employed on a part-time basis).

Two subjects (9%) reported a complete change in direction in career. One of these interpreters commented, "[I] Cannot risk further damage to my arms. Looking at a shorter working life in this area—so diversifying skills." (I 19, male signed language interpreter, employed on a full-time basis).

In terms of change in employment status due to OOS, 15 of the 23 subjects (65%) reported that they continued to work in the usual job, with no changes; 3 (13%) had been redeployed to different duties and commented:

- I monitor hours to be worked (I 77, female signed language interpreter, employed on a part-time basis);
- I changed my job which mostly involves readback and do a bit of freelance (I 79, female signed language interpreter, employed on a full-time basis); and
- Now do little freelance (I 82, female signed language interpreter, not working).

Two subjects had left the work force primarily due to OOS, and one interpreter had left the field for other reasons. (One interpreter did not select an option on the questionnaire, but wrote the comment "I monitor hours worked." The last of the interpreters who had a diagnosed OOS condition did not respond to this question at all.) The responses reported

TABLE 12. *Contingency Table of Prevalence of OOS and Work Duration*

	<1	1 – 2	2 – 3	3 – 4	>4	Total
OOS	2	1	3	4	4	14
No OOS	8	10	16	12	8	54
Total	10	11	19	16	12	68

above indicate that a quarter (26%) of the subjects had modified their career goals due to the experience of OOS. Comments made during interviews give an indication of the sorts of modifications which have been made:

It has made me a little cautious about interpreting but made me not want to stop it. I like to be careful about the environment in which I interpret and my own health. I try to do exercises, but I don't do them well enough or often enough. (I 80, male signed language interpreter, employed on a full-time basis, has a diagnosed OOS condition)

I'm just taking each day as it comes at the moment, but you always think, "What if it goes too long and what if I can't go to work or what if I have to do something else?" . . . I've become more acutely aware of interpreters' needs in general ... I don't dislike the job because of it, all these terrible things that have happened to interpreters and in the back of your mind you think, "Can I keep doing this?" . . . You think, "Probably not, and if not, what am I going to do, because I can't do anything else." (I 2, female signed language interpreter, employed on a full-time basis, has a diagnosed OOS condition)

Two years ago (before I was injured), I saw the whole thing as a great challenge, that I could go in and play with a spoken language, and change it into a three dimensional thing, and come out with really good words. I loved the mind play. The challenge for me now is to be more assertive in what I accept from other people and what I am prepared for them asking of me, to assert what my rights are, as an interpreter. It's very, very hard. The crux of it is about guilt obligations for me to overcome at the moment. . . . We push ourselves, we allow it to happen. I think there is a danger that we sort of have to better ourselves, and we push and push in that regard. We never hit a point where we think, "OK, well that's fine, you're doing a good job now".

TABLE 13. *Level of Effect of Interpreting on Three Aspects of Life (All Subjects)*

Effect	Very strong		Strong		None		Little		Very little		Not sure		Do not wish to reply	
	OOS	No OOS	OOS	No OOS	OOS	No OOS	OOS	No OOS	OOS	No OOS	OOS	No OOS	OOS	No OOS
Personal Relationships	8 (38%)	13 (62%)	10 (25%)	28 (70%)	1 (8%)	11 (92%)	2 (11%)	16 (88%)	1 (10%)	8 (80%)	0	0	0	2
Family Life	9 (35%)	17 (65%)	8 (22%)	26 (72%)	1 (9%)	10 (91%)	3 (14%)	18 (82%)	1 (17%)	5 (83%)	0	0	0	2
Social Life	2 (12%)	14 (82%)	12 (35%)	20 (59%)	2 (10%)	9 (90%)	6 (26%)	17 (74%)	0	6	0	0	0	2

(I 136, female signed language interpreter, employed on a part-time basis, has a diagnosed OOS condition)

When asked if they wished to continue working in their present position, seven of the OOS sufferers responded, "yes"; none responded in the negative, one subject was not sure, and one did not wish to comment. Among the reasons given for wishing to continue were:

- challenge and personal satisfaction (I 77, female signed language interpreter, employed on a contract basis);
- because it is worthwhile and I learn (I 79, female signed language interpreter, employed on a full-time basis);
- I am able to balance my workload to minimise the pain in my arm. I enjoy my work immensely and do not wish to work in a different field (I 87, female signed language interpreter, employed on a part-time basis); and
- it's a responsible position (I 98, female signed language interpreter, employed on a part-time basis).

DISCUSSION

Hypothesis 1: Women Will Be Worse Affected by OOS Than Men

As reported earlier, 20% of the male subjects (5 out of 25) and 22% of the females (18 out of 81) in this sample suffer from OOS. The results of the chi square analysis show that there is no indication that females are significantly more likely to suffer OOS in this occupation. This hypothesis is not supported. It can therefore be postulated that signed language interpreters are affected by overuse injuries due to poor work organization, rather than as a result of gender (i.e., because one gender is weaker or stronger than the other).

Hypothesis 2: Interpreters Who Have Worked for a Greater Number of Years Will Be More Severely Affected by OOS Than Those New to the Occupation

As the prevalence of OOS is lower for the less-experienced group (12% for those who have been in the field for up to three years) and higher among those who have been engaged in employment for a longer period of time (68% for those who have been employed for up to nine years), it appears that length of time in the occupation is correlated with OOS development. Results from the chi square analysis do not support this hypothesis. It can therefore be postulated that signed language interpreters are affected by overuse injuries due to work intensification and poor work organization, regardless of how long they have been employed.

It is interesting to note that the prevalence of OOS declined in the group of interpreters who had been in the occupation the longest (more than nine years). It appears that some injured interpreters may have chosen to leave the field entirely, as at least two of the interpreters surveyed reported that they had left interpreting because of an overuse injury.

Hypothesis 3: Part-Time or Freelance Workers Will Be Worse Affected by OOS Than Full-Time Workers

As 27% of the full-time workers and 18% of the part-time employees suffer from OOS, it appears that there is a more significant link between full-time work and increased likelihood of OOS than for part-time work.

However, chi square analysis indicated that the relationship between employment tenure and development of OOS was not significant. Therefore, this hypothesis was not supported.

Greater workloads, extended interpreting sessions without breaks, and work pressures for full-time employees may be the reason for the higher prevalence in that group. Many part-time and casual employees reported a feeling of freedom to "pick and choose" interpreting assignments as they suited, whereas full-time employees may be unable to exercise a similar level of choice.

Hypothesis 4: Interpreters Who Work for Long Periods at a Time Will Be Worse Affected Than Those Working Short Periods

All interpreters (with the exception of two individuals who are currently away from the work force) reported that they interpreted for a varying number of hours each week. The number of days worked per week varied from one to five, and the hours worked each day varied from two to five.

Data displayed in Table 13 show a complex pattern of combinations of days worked per week and hours worked per day. Finding evidence to support this hypothesis is therefore quite complicated due to the wide range of working conditions of the subjects. Results from chi square analysis indicated a nonsignificant relationship between the presence of OOS and periods worked. This hypothesis could not be disproved.

Although no statistically significant relationships emerged in the data, strong trends are evident in some areas, and it seems reasonable to draw the overall conclusion from the quantitative and qualitative data that the interpreters most at risk of developing OOS are those who interpret for more than four hours per day and have been in the field for more than seven years, regardless of whether they are employed on a full- or part-time basis.

It also appears that interpreters are highly motivated to remain in the field despite (in some cases) quite severe pain. Feelings of personal satisfaction and enjoyment appear to outweigh the negative aspects of pain. Such comments need to be viewed in light of the high levels of job commitment generally among caring workers, the feminization of interpreting work, and the generally low levels of ambition or career path goals described by interviewees.

The way in which signed language interpreting is organized has great potential for creating stress. As described earlier, interpreting work has repetitive aspects, not only in content (e.g., the recurring need that interpreters reported to negotiate seating position and break times for almost every assignment), but also in the limited range of physical movement involved. In addition, interpreting places extremely high cognitive and physical demands upon the interpreter. Stress for a signed language interpreter may be caused by a combination of these factors and others, such as low participation in decision-making and low rates of pay.

The final stage of this study focuses on the prevention of OOS in signed language interpreters, through consultation with workers and development of safe work practices and conditions.

CONCLUSION, IMPLICATIONS, AND RECOMMENDATIONS

The data gathered in this study clearly show that OOS is a significant occupational health risk for signed language interpreters in Australia. Roughly one-third (32%) of the interpreters in this study have either been medically diagnosed (22%) or suffer from symptoms indicative of overuse injury (10%).

There appears to be no difference in injury rates on the basis of gender (20% of males and 22% of females in this study have a medically diagnosed injury) or number of years in the field, or indeed the individual duration of each interpreting day. Therefore it can be said that it is the organization and process of work for interpreters which must change to reduce the incidence of OOS. The recommendations below focus on preventive strategies.

Signed language interpreters who wish to remain in the occupation on either a full-time or part-time basis need to be mindful of the hazards associated with their work. This is not only the individual's responsibility, but also (and primarily) that of management. Legally, there are primary prevention requirements placed on management in Queensland and other Australian states and territories. Obligations on an employer are imposed to ensure the health and safety of each of the workers in the workplace. An employer is also obligated to ensure a safe place and process of work for each worker.

A primary obligation imposed by the Workplace Health and Safety Act is that of "Duty of Care." The Duty of Care requires that everything "reasonably practicable" be done to protect the health and safety of all those at the workplace. This duty is placed on all employers, manufacturers, and suppliers; their employees; and any others who may have an influence on the hazards in a workplace. Specific employer duties flow from the duty of care. These include:

1. Provision and maintenance of a safe plant;
2. Safe systems of work;
3. A safe working environment and adequate welfare facilities;
4. Information and instruction on workplace hazards and supervision of employees in safe work practices;
5. Monitoring the health and safety of employees and related record keeping;
6. Employment of qualified persons to provide health and safety advice;
7. Nomination of a senior employer representative; and
8. Monitoring conditions at any workplace under their control and management.

As yet, organizations employing interpreters have not been subject to severe penalties under OHS law. Unfortunately, because of the employment situation (i.e., usually part-time and insecure), status (professionally unrecognized group), and gender-based socialization pressures (i.e., caring professional more committed to client than self), affected individuals are unlikely to feel able to speak out and overcome covert pressure to not report injuries. However, under both statute and common law, the primary responsibility of the employer is clear. The common law basis of predictability and preventability, and the nexus between cause and effect can provide the basis by which a common law prosecution could be readily won by an interpreter. Several states in Australia have awarded significant compensation to workers suffering from occupationally related OOS as well as stress. Yet to date, successful common law claims are rare amongst interpreters.

The keys to the alleviation of OOS as a major problem for signed language interpreters appear to be prevention, early diagnosis, and effective management. With such approaches, if early warning signs do appear, the process can be interrupted and injury prevented from progressing to chronic disability, possible unemployment; and economic loss for the interpreter, followed by significant court-imposed costs for employers should litigation ensue. Education for recognition of early detection of warning signs is recommended for all interpreters. This recommendation stems from the data reported above, indicating that a number of interpreters who experienced difficulties with everyday tasks did not seek medical advice.

However, as also stated above, the best treatment for OOS is to ensure that it does not arise in the first place. In the early stages of OOS, treatment is theoretically simple and effective: immediate rest of the affected limb, which should be completely pain-free before the worker returns to work. Unfortunately, as was seen in the interview data, this early opportunity for rest is often lost because the injury has not been properly diagnosed, the sufferer cannot afford to take the necessary time off work, or he or she does not dare to admit to an injury, which would make the interpreter inefficient in management's eyes.

Rather than concentrating on treatment of syndromes already established, the only really acceptable health and safety policy for signed language interpreters is one based on prevention, which means dealing with the labor process causes of OOS at the source by modifying the workplace and/or work processes to remove those causes or reduce their influence. To prevent OOS developing in initial stages, specific guidelines must be enforced; for example, set amounts of exposure time and regular breaks during interpreting work. When initial symptoms present, a required recuperation period must be set, during which entirely different tasks are performed, so that the affected limbs/ligaments/muscles are rested. If even mild pain continues, the affected joint or part of the body must be rested immediately. This does not always mean that the worker must take time off work: He or she may be given other work to do which involves the use of different muscles.

Supervisors should also undertake training in occupational health and safety. Often supervisors and fellow workers become aware too late that a worker is experiencing distress. Symptoms are sometimes observed through the worker cradling arms, constantly rubbing the hands or wrists, or taking unexplained short absences from work. It is important that these early warning signs be noticed and acted upon. Workers should be encouraged to report symptoms early. They should feel they are able to report promptly without anxiety-producing procedures, and certainly punitive measures should not exist (either covert or overt). Workers will need to be reassured that reporting will not result in victim-blaming, work loss, or income reduction.

Tackling OOS is a complex task, and it must be done in a systematic and professional way. The following recommendations are predicated in light of causal relationships that can be justified by the data, but they are not exclusive of other plausible and untested explanations. The following list provides both a summary and a reminder of the issues with which management needs to deal. It is important to bear in mind that further research is needed in order to better understand the direct and indirect causes of OOS. Such research would also serve to qualify the efficacy of these recommendations:

Physical Environment

1. High standards of health and safety must be achieved, maintained, and monitored. Employers should consult Australian Standards with regard to appropriate lighting, seating, and other requirements for all employees, including interpreters.
2. The physical environment in which the person works should offer comfort on all levels—physical, emotional, and mental.
3. Work should be arranged so that the interpreter is able to change positions and stretch while interpreting (i.e., to cradle hands when standing, quickly massage hands and arms, and drop the arms to the sides while seated). Changing hand dominance is not recommended, because the problem will probably develop in the other limb more quickly.
4. Interpreters should not be seated under air-conditioning vents or in a drafty position.

Equipment

1. Desks, chairs, and other furniture used by interpreters must be ergonomically correct and adjustable for each individual.
2. Workers should be taught ergonomic principles associated with furniture or equipment and ways of making adjustments.

Job Content

1. The job of an interpreter should, wherever possible, lead to a career path or differentiation of working conditions.

2. Employers should provide opportunities which enable workers to contribute to decisions affecting their jobs and the goals of the organization.

3. The employer should ensure that the goals of the organization and the clients' expectations are clear. As far as signed language interpreters are concerned, the education of Deaf and hearing consumers as to the role of the interpreter is considered important.

4. The employer must accept the responsibility to provide training and information to ensure the interpreter is able to perform at acceptable levels. This information should include occupational health and safety guidelines as well as provisions for interpreting skill development.

5. Work tasks should include the ability to provide feedback on performance in a number of dimensions both directly and through others. Positive criticism, standards monitoring, and a debriefing officer should also be utilized.

The need for a debriefing mechanism was stated by many interpreters during their interviews. Many individuals expressed a strong need to discuss specific types of interpreting jobs, particularly those of a highly emotional nature, such as murder or sexual abuse trials or medical situations where the Deaf person has been given notice of a serious or life-threatening condition. The need for a confidential and effective method to deal with the emotional stress of such interpreting work was clearly expressed.

6. Interpreters could also have a supervisor or colleague observe work habits to make suggestions about posture and sign and fingerspelling formation to assist in developing and maintaining healthy work practices.

7. The employer should also aim to provide a mix of assignments, so that interpreters are not constantly called upon to perform highly taxing assignments.

Management Style and Structure

1. Employers need to provide more comprehensive programs or manuals, which form an integral part of their OHS management system. Alternatively, they should supplement manuals

with pamphlets focusing on specific work tasks (Mayhew, Quinlan, & Bennett, 1996, p. 143).

2. Acknowledgment of the value of the human contribution to the organization is important. The individual interpreter should be consulted and involved in decisions about the type of work he or she undertakes.

3. The employer should provide clear, well-communicated objectives, specific strategies, induction, and training and adopt a consistent approach to dealing with staff. Effective communication can be established through a program of regular staff meetings combined with interpreter newsletters.

4. The employer should attempt to provide enough flexibility to allow individuals a degree of control over variety in their jobs. The key to this approach is management adopting a safe system of work rather than encouraging interpreters to accept sole responsibility for their own health and safety. This may well save the employer a substantial OHS fine later.

5. Employers should nominate a person or persons responsible for safety and give undertakings in relation to monitoring and rectifying hazards. A Workplace Health and Safety Committee should be established in each workplace in accordance with Workplace Health and Safety legislation. In the case of interpreters, such undertakings will involve liaison, consultation, and education of consumers of interpreting services.

6. Interpreting service coordinators, managers, and other staff must all be fully informed of their OHS obligations in relation to the assignments that interpreters undertake.

7. The management of the deploying agency must accept responsibility to make sure that all the above obligations are being effectively met.

8. Organizations should change the status of interpreters from casual to permanent part- or full-time employees with a career structure. This could be achieved through the establishment of a workplace consultative committee, comprising representatives of management, employers, and (ideally) ASLIA. The consultative committee would negotiate on terms and conditions of permanent employment, as well as the number of positions available.

Recruitment and Selection Procedures

1. In recruitment of interpreters, it is essential to match the job requirements with the skills, knowledge, and experience of the applicants.

2. Employers should provide formal induction programs for new interpreters, which outline the OHS features of their management system.

3. Employers should provide incentives, which will enhance the skills of interpreters. In the government sector, strong support should be provided for the professionalization of interpreting, in the shape of formal training and education.

4. Employers should look for guidance in developing recruitment policies. The policies and guidelines developed by ASLIA are a valuable starting point.

Training Arrangements

1. Employers should provide regular opportunities for personal and professional skill development, particularly in the area of vocabulary development and language use in specific settings, such as legal, medical, and educational. The need for professional skill development was a clearly identified need among all the subjects in this study, particularly interpreters (formerly known as level 3 interpreters). Interpreters at this level often feel that they give much of their time to assisting and training paraprofessional interpreters without being provided with opportunities for advancement themselves.

2. The aim of training is to fill in any gaps in the skills, knowledge, and experience of the individual and to instruct the worker in the skills required in order to do the job well. Initial training for interpreters should be of sufficient duration to permit interpreters to increase their hand and wrist strength. This in turn may help protect against the risks of developing OOS from interpreting tasks.

3. The employer must accept the responsibility to provide training and information to ensure the interpreter is able to perform at acceptable levels. This information should include occupational health and safety guidelines as well as provisions for interpreting skill development.

4. Employers of interpreters must be made aware of their primary legal responsibility to prevent injuries to their employees.

5. Job rotation principles and time/task sharing should be routinely scheduled. Interpreters should be given information on work hazards (such as repetition injuries, postural and ergonomic problems, etc.) and preventative strategies, including the importance of taking adequate rest breaks and warming up prior to work in the same way as an athlete does. The key to this approach is management adopting a safe system of work rather than encouraging employees to accept sole responsibility for their own health and safety.

6. Employers should consider adopting systems of paid educational leave whereby workers are entitled to a certain amount of time off on full pay to pursue training courses. Alternatively, the employer could provide sponsored in-house training.

Hours of Work

1. Employers should strive to establish a human environment at work rather than a production process of interpreting. Guidelines that set out an appropriate duration of work for interpreters on a daily and weekly basis urgently need to be established. Employers should work with interpreters and consumers to establish these guidelines.

2. It is recommended that interpreters work no more than 25 hours per week in actual interpreting. If in an educational setting, the number of hours per week worked should not exceed 20, and interpreting work should always be worked in a team arrangement.

3. Any interpreter who works for more than four out of seven days per week must not work more than five hours a day on those days. Interpreters working three days of the week or less may work seven hours a day, but only if working with a partner.

These two recommendations are a response to clear evidence from the questionnaire data demonstrating that the majority of the interpreters who suffered an OOS injury reported that they worked four or more days a week (12 interpreters out of 19), and of this group, 5 worked more than four hours on each of these days.

4. Rest breaks must be built into an interpreter's workday. Interpreters must not work more than 30 minutes without a break (which should be of at least 10 minutes duration). The breaks depend upon a number of factors, including:

   - The physical and mental demands of the task;
   - The environment; and
   - The needs of the individual interpreter.

5. Rest breaks must be taken before the onset of fatigue, rather than as recuperative periods. Frequent short breaks are preferable to longer, infrequent breaks.

6. Two interpreters must be sent to any interpreting assignment of greater than two hours duration. Two interpreters working in a team should not work more than seven hours in a day. A seven-hour workday must be broken by a 15-minute break in the first half and second half of the day, as well as a meal break of at least 45 minutes duration in the middle of the day.

7. During periods of high demand, management should take care not to overload workers and exceed the above recommendations, even for brief periods of time.

Recognition of Other Service Condition Matters

1. Payments systems and wage levels must be established, which are seen to be fair and reflect the skills and contributions of individuals to the organization. At present, there are pay scales which differentiate between different levels of accreditation for signed language interpreters. However, there is no consistency in these rates across the country, and no differentiation within groups (i.e., an interpreter of five years experience is paid the same hourly rate as a recently accredited interpreter). Likewise, a paraprofessional interpreter working at a tertiary education institution (where highly technical language may be interpreted) is paid the same as one working in a primary or secondary school. The rates of pay are also applied differentially, according to the interpreter's status in the organization (either full- or part-time).

2. A system needs to be established that recognizes shift working and work during unsocial hours. Penalty payments for week-

end or evening work should also be considered. Interpreters in this study generally reported lack of satisfaction with pay levels.

3. Consideration should be given to the amount, the pay levels, and the choice of when holidays can be taken. All workers returning from leave of any kind should be given time to adjust to repetitive tasks again. More rest breaks than usual should be taken during the first week back from leave.

4. Procedures need to be developed for dealing with grievances, complaints, discipline, and dismissals, and these must be seen to be fair. Systems for reporting grievances (either from interpreters themselves or from clients) must be developed in consultation with interpreters and disseminated and used widely. ASLIA policies could be used as a starting point.

   As many interpreters work in isolation, away from the security of a regular daily workplace, sound performance management systems must be implemented to provide inter-preters with constructive feedback to assist in their profes-sional development. Discipline and dismissal procedures must be in line with what is required under industrial relations legislation (i.e., a "three strikes" policy).

5. Workers' compensation, superannuation, and long service leave should also be considered.

The strength and support of a trade union may be essential if workers are to challenge the root causes of OOS. However, no single trade union exists for interpreters. Individuals who have OOS are easily isolated and victimized. Approaches by individual members of a work force are un-likely to get very far when the whole system of work needs to be re-viewed and changed, and demands by an individual worker are likely to be met with hostility. Trade unionists can demand consultation on how work is done. However the role of an elected Workplace Health and Safety representative is currently restricted. Thus under Queensland law, the Workplace Health and Safety officer is of core importance in protect-ing the OHS of interpreters. Health and safety rights and practices en-shrined in the legislation should ensure that OOS never occurs in the first place. However, development of codes of practice and legislative reforms have favored male work domains, which are strongly unionized. Fre-quently, the nomination of a Workplace Health and Safety representative is a token gesture to fulfil legislative obligations. It is common to find men dominating powerful decision-making positions in agencies dealing with OHS, such as in industry committees, government bodies, professional associations, and unions (Forrester, 1992, p. 115).

As no union currently exists for interpreters, the best way to start may be for interpreters to talk to their colleagues to determine common areas of concern and devise a list of legislative breaches with which to meet with management. The following are some basic conditions which can be discussed with management.

1. An undertaking from management that all work procedures will be reviewed to identify factors causing OOS. (In all Australian states and territories, owners and/or managers are required to provide a workplace and process of labor that is without risk under the Workplace Health and Safety Act.)

2. A commitment to implement the changes necessary to prevent the occurrence of injuries.

3. An agreement that a clear timetable will be drawn up for the review and implementation of changes.

4. A commitment to provide ongoing education/training for at-risk supervisors, management, and workers in OOS prevention and case handling.

5. Development of a clear system for the early reporting of OOS symptoms by workers, including the use of an injury log book.

6. An agreement that all people with symptoms and signs of OOS will be moved to other work or be given time off to rest the affected joint or limb without loss of pay, conditions, status, or other benefits.

7. An agreement for a minimum 10-minute rest break to be taken after every 30 minutes of continuous repetitive work, in addition to tea and meal breaks.

Many of the above principles are not adhered to in spheres of caring work, such as signed language interpreting, which are largely populated by women. Historically, female injuries have attracted less attention than male injuries, possibly because women were not seen to be workers in the same sense as men, and because so many injuries went unreported.

The legislative reliance on self-regulation is seriously misplaced as it assumes workers and employers are equally knowledgeable about threats to health and well-being and that they can actually do anything about the exposure to identified hazards such as repetitive movements over prolonged periods of time. Such misplaced beliefs in the efficacy of the law can have quite serious effects upon less-powerful women workers.

What may be required is for an interpreter to achieve a legal "win" in the courts as a test case of employer liability. If such a case were well publicized, it may have the effect of giving a severe shock to other employers, particularly if a custodial sentence (one year, possible under the Act for causing bodily harm) were imposed.

In sum, OOS problems should be prevented by:

- Sound OHS management of the labor process of interpreting work, including "warming up" to the task;
- Ensuring that workers are provided with appropriate equipment and are educated about and adopt comfortable, correct postures when working;
- Varying the types of jobs or the way in which they are performed;
- Realizing that if soreness, pain, or other symptoms become noticeable, rest for the sore part of the body and reporting of symptoms to the appropriate person as soon as possible are essential; and
- Removing overt or covert threats to recognition of the problem.

Management should seek to develop an environment in which consideration has been given to the physical consequences of interpreting work and sound occupational health practices are put into place. Workers need to feel that their health and safety are given high priority and that they may report concerns promptly and confidently. This is not likely to happen until people feel secure enough in their employment, are aware of their rights, and realize management procedures (rather than injured workers) are the root cause of overuse injury. When these things happen, workers will start refusing to do the jobs that are draining them and ruining their mental and physical health.

REFERENCES

Adams, M. (1971). The compassion trap. In V. Gornick & B. K. Moran (Eds.), *Women in sexist society: Studies in power and powerlessness*. New York: Basic Books.

Australian Bureau of Statistics. (1998). *Employee earnings and hours, May, Australia Catalogue Number 6305.0*. Canberra: Australian Bureau of Statistics.

Australian Sign Language Interpreters' Association. (1998). *Strategic Plan version 2.0*. N.p.: Australian Sign Language Interpreters' Association.

Bammer, G. (1990). The epidemic is over . . . or is it? *Australian Society,* April 22–24.

Bammer, G., & Blignault, I. (1988). More than a pain in the arms: A review of the consequences of developing OOSs. *Journal of Occupational Health and Safety Australia and New Zealand, 4* (5), 389–397.

Beard, K. M., & Edwards, J. R. (1995). Employees at risk: Contingent work and the psychological experience of contingent workers. In C. L. Cooper & D. M. Rousseau (Eds.), *Trends in organisational behaviour* (Volume 2). New York: John Wiley & Sons.

Beechey, V. (1987). *Unequal work*. London: Verso.

Bennett, L. (1994). Women and enterprise bargaining: The legal and institutional framework. *Journal of Industrial Relations, 36* (2), 191–212.

Boreham, R., Hall, R., Harley, B., & Whitehouse, G. (1996). What does enterprise bargaining mean for gender equity? Some empirical evidence. *Labour and Industry 7* (1), 51–68.

Bradley, H. (1999). *Gender and power in the workplace: Analysing the impact of economic change*. London: Macmillan.

Brill, N. L. (1990). *Working with people—The helping process*. New York: Longman.

Brosnan, P. & Underhill, E. (1998). Introduction: Precarious employment. *Labour and Industry, 8* (3), 1–4.

Browne, C. D., Nolan, B. M., & Faithfull, D. K. (1987). Occupational repetition strain injuries. *The Medical Journal of Australia, 140*, 329–332.

Caudron, S. (1994). Contingent workforce spurs HR planning. *Personnel Journal, 73*, 52–60.

Cergol, S. (1991). Repetitive motion injury. *NTID Focus*, (Winter/Spring), 12–16.

Charmaz, K. (1983). Loss of self: A fundamental form of suffering in the chronically ill. *Sociology of Health and Illness, 5* (2), 34–39.

Cohn, L., Lowry, R. M., & Hart, S. (1990). Overuse syndromes of the upper extremity in interpreters for the Deaf. *Orthopedics, 13* (2), 207–209.

DeCaro, J. J., Feuerstein, M., & Hurwitz, T. A. (1992). Cumulative trauma disorders among educational interpreters. *American Annals of the Deaf,* *137* (3), 288–292.

Epstein, C. F. (1987). Multiple demands and multiple roles: The conditions of successful management. In F. J. Crosby (Ed.), *Spouse, parent, worker: On gender and multiple roles.* London: Yale University Press.

Ewan, C., Lowy, E., & Reid, J. (1991). "Falling out of culture": The effects of repetition strain injury on sufferers' roles and identity. *Sociology of Health and Illness, 13* (2), 168–192.

Feuerstein, M. & Fitzgerald, T. E. (1992). Biomechanical factors affecting upper extremity cumulative trauma disorder in sign language interpreters. *Journal of Medicine, 34* (3), 257–264.

Finch, J. & Groves, D. (Eds.). (1983). *A labour of love: Women, work and caring.* London: Routledge & Kegan Paul.

Fine, B. (1992). *Women's employment and the capitalist family.* London: Routledge.

Forrest, A. (1973). The condition of the poor in revolutionary Bordeaux. *Past and Present, 59,* 151–152.

Forrester, C. (1992). Preventative strategies: The costs. In D. Blackmur, D. Fingleton, & D. Akers (Eds.), *Women's occupational health and safety: The unmet needs. Papers from the forum on women's occupational health and safety.* Brisbane, Australia: Women's Consultative Council and Queensland University of Technology.

Fowkles, M. R. (1987). Role combinations and role conflict: Introductory perspective. In Crosby, F. J. (Ed.), *Spouse, parent, worker: On gender and multiple roles.* London: Yale University Press.

Fry, H. J. (1986). Overuse syndrome in musicians 100 years ago. *The Medical Journal of Australia, 145,* 620–625.

Game, A. & Pringle, R. (1983). *Gender at work.* Sydney, Australia: George Allen and Unwin.

Gamst, F. C. (Ed.). (1995). *Meanings of work: Considerations for the twenty first century.* Albany, New York: State University of New York Press

Graham, H. (1991). The concept of caring in feminist research: The case of domestic service. *Sociology, 25* (1), 61–78.

Grint, K. (1991). *The sociology of work: An introduction.* Cambridge, England: Polity Press.

Hall, R. (1986). *Dimensions of work.* London: Sage.

Heiler, K. (1994). *Enterprise bargaining: Implications for occupational health and safety.* ACIRRT Working Paper No. 34. Sydney, Australia: Australian Centre for Industrial Relations Research and Teaching.

Heiler, K. (1996). *Is enterprise bargaining good for your health?* ACIRRT Monograph No. 14. Sydney, Australia: Australian Centre for Industrial Relations Research and Teaching.

Hopkins, A. (1989). The social construction of repetition strain injury. *Australian and New Zealand Journal of Sociology, 25* (2), 239–259.

Hufton, O. (1971). Women in revolution 1789–1796. *Past and Present, 53,* 92.

Kurppa, K., Viikari-Juntura, E., Kuosma, E., Huuskonen, M., & Kivi, P. (1991). Incidence of tenosynovitis or peritendinitis and epicondylitis in a meat-processing factory. *Scandinavian Journal of Work and Environmental Health, 17* (1), 32–37.

Lansbury, R. D. & Kitay, J. (1997). Toward new employment relations: Continuity, change and diversity. In J. Kitay & R. D. Lansbury (Eds.). *Changing employment relations.* Oxford, England: Oxford University Press.

McDermott, F. T. (1989). Repetition strain injury: A review of current understanding. *Medical Journal of Australia, 144,* 196–200.

Mayhew, C. (1996). The endangered proletariat: occupational injury amongst sub-contractors and consultants. *Labour and Industry, 7* (1), 149–164.

Mayhew, C. & Quinlan, M. (1998). *Outsourcing and occupational health and safety: A comparative study of factory-based and outworkers in the Australian TCF industry.* UNSW Studies in Australian Industrial Relations, No. 40. Sydney: Industrial Relations Research Centre, University of New South Wales.

Mayhew, C., Quinlan, M., & Bennett, L. (1996). *The effects of subcontracting/outsourcing on occupational health and safety.* Sydney: NSW Industrial Relations Research Centre, University of New South Wales.

Meals, R. A., Payne, W., & Gaines, R. (1988). Functional demands and consequences of manual communication. *The Journal of Hand Surgery, 13A* (5), 686–691.

Meekosha, H. & Jakubowicz, A. (1986). Women suffering RSI: The hidden relations of gender, the labour process and medicine. *Journal of Occupational Health and Safety Australia and New Zealand, 2* (5), 390–401.

Moore, A., Wells, R., & Ranney, D. (1991). Quantifying exposure in occupational manual tasks with cumulative trauma disorder potential. *Ergonomics, 34* (12), 1433–1453.

Mullaly, J. & Grigg, L. (1988). RSI: Integrating the major theories. *Australian Journal of Psychology, 40* (1), 19–33.

National Accreditation Authority for Translators and Interpreters (NAATI). (1991). *Directory of Language Aides, Translators and Interpreters.* Canberra, Australia, NAATI.

Novarra, V. (1980). *Women's work, men's work: The ambivalence of equality.* London: Martin Boyars.

Ozolins, U. & Bridge, M. (1999). *Sign language interpreting in Australia.* Melbourne, Australia: Language Australia.

Pahl, R. E. (1984). *Divisions of labour.* Oxford, England: Basil Blackwell.

Peitchinis, S. G. (1989). *Women at work—Discrimination and response.*
Toronto, Canada: McCelland & Stewart.

Pennington, S. & Westover, B. (1989). *A hidden workforce: Homeworkers in England 1850–1985.* London: MacMillan.

Pfeffer, J. & Baron, J. N. (1988). Taking the workers back out: Recent trends in the structuring of employment. In B. M. Staw & L. L. Cummings (Eds.). *Research in organisational behaviour.* Greenwich, CT: JAI Press.

Polivka, A. E. & Nardone, T. (1989). On the definition of contingent work. *Monthly Labour Review, 112,* 9–16.

Probert, B. (1990). *Working life* Victoria, Australia: Penguin, Ringwood.

Probert, B. & Wilson, B. (Eds.). (1993). *Pink collar blues: Work, gender and technology.* Carlton, Australia: Melbourne University Press.

Quinlan, M. (1992). Women's occupational health and safety: a conceptual framework. In D. Blackmur, D. Fingleton, & D. Akers (Eds.). *Women's occupational health and safety: The unmet needs.* Papers from the forum on Women's occupational health and safety. Brisbane, Australia: Women's Consultative Council and Queensland University of Technology.

Rempel, D. M., Harrison, R. J., & Barnhart, S. (1992). Work-related cumulative trauma disorders of the upper extremity. *Journal of the American Medical Association, 267* (6), 838–842.

Sanderson, G. (1987). *Overuse syndrome among sign language interpreters.* Silver Spring, Maryland: RID Publications.

Sayer, A. & Walker, R. (1992). *The new social economy: Re-working the division of labour.* Cambridge, England: Blackwell.

Scott, H. (1984). *Working your way to the bottom: The feminization of poverty.* London: Pandora Press.

Scott, J. W. & Tilly, L. A. (1975). Women's work and the family in nineteenth century Europe. In A. H. Amsden (Ed.). *The economics of women and work.* Harmondsworth, UK: Penguin.

Scott, J. W. & Tilly, L. A. (1978). *Women, work, and family.* New York: Holt, Rinehart, and Winston.

Shadbolt, B. (1988). The severity of life strains and stresses reported by female OOS sufferers. *Journal of Occupational Health and Safety Australia and New Zealand, 4* (3), 239–249.

Standards Association of Australia. (1987). *Occupational overuse syndrome—Preventative guidelines.* North Sydney, Australia: Standards Association of Australia.

Statham, A., Muller, E. M., & Mauksch, H. O. (Eds.). (1988). *The worth of women's work.* Albany, New York: State University of New York Press.

Stedt, J. D. (1989). Carpal tunnel syndrome: the risk to educational interpreters. *American Annals of the Deaf, 134* (3), 223–226.

Summers, A. (1994). *Damned whores and God's police.* Ringwood, UK: Penguin.

Waersted, M., & Westgaard, R. H. (1991). Working hours as a risk factor in the development of musculoskeletal complaints. *Ergonomics, 34* (3), 265–276.

Wharton, A. S. (1993). The affective consequences of service work—Managing emotions on the job. *Work and Occupations,* 20 (2), 205–232.

Williams, C. (1988). *Blue, white and pink collar workers in Australia—Technicians, bank employees and flight attendants.* Sydney, Australia: Allen and Unwin.

Williams, C. & Thorpe, B. (1992). *Beyond industrial sociology: The work of men and women.* North Sydney, Australia: Allen and Unwin.

Workplace Health and Safety Act (1986). *Queensland Government Printer.*

Attitudes of Deaf Leaders Toward

Signed Language Interpreters and Interpreting

Lawrence Forestal

Elderly deaf leaders who witnessed the emergence of signed language interpreting as a paid profession in the 1960s were inclined to view interpreters as friends and/or protectors of deaf people. The then newly paid profession of interpreting caught many elderly deaf persons unprepared because they were used to getting services gratis. For instance, they had used their relatives, teachers, or ministers as voluntary interpreters for many years (Gannon, 1981; Schein, 1981; Stewart et al., 1998).

On the other hand, young deaf leaders who have had childhood experiences of dealing with interpreters in local public schools, colleges, and/ or universities, as mandated by Section 504 under the 1973 Vocational Rehabilitation Act and the Individuals with Disabilities Education Act (IDEA), might tend to view interpreters as strictly communication facilitators. They may not be always friendly to interpreters. Young deaf individuals have been generally accustomed to the idea of having interpreters as a necessary part of their lives, for example, in mainstream education. It is more likely that they are critical about the quality of interpreters and hold strong feelings about interpreting issues because professional interpreters deliver a paid service (Gannon, 1981; Schein, 1981; Stewart et al., 1998).

In 1994, a National Association of the Deaf-Registry of Interpreters for the Deaf (NAD-RID) Task Force, now known as the National Council on Interpreting (NCI), was established to resolve interpreter-related problems and concerns. NCI supports the concept of developing one joint testing instrument for sign language interpreters based on the strengths of the tests designed by NAD and RID (Nettles, 1996a, 1996b). In November 2002, NAD announced the creation of its National Interpreter Certification (NIC) program, which will work with RID and NCI to develop a joint interpreter testing and certification system, which will ultimately become the national standard.

Interpreting is one of the primary support services for deaf people. Yet, there has been evidence that deaf people have a level of dissatisfaction with interpreters and interpreting. Actions taken by the RID and the NAD have tried to address this perceived dissatisfaction since the late 1980s. However, there has been no empirical data documenting deaf people's attitudes about interpreters and interpreting, that is, their feelings, beliefs, and reactions to interpreters and interpreting. Such data have always been needed to enhance efforts to improve interpreting services to the deaf population.

In order to address this lack, the current study focuses on the attitudes of American deaf leaders. Toward this objective, an attitude scale was developed and tested with a sample of deaf leaders. Factors possibly influencing the attitudes of the leaders, such as gender, age, education, frequency of interpreter use, and their varied experiences with interpreters, were assessed.

METHODOLOGY

This chapter describes the results of an exploratory study of deaf leaders' attitudes toward sign language interpreters and interpreting in general. Research questions include:

1. Do attitudes vary with the age of deaf leaders?
2. Are the frequency of interpreter use and the incidence of negative experiences with interpreters associated with the leaders' attitudes?
3. Do the views of female and male leaders differ?
4. Do the educational levels of deaf leaders influence their attitudes?

The leaders were elected by fellow members and respectively represented the interests of their national and state associations of the deaf.

An initial mailing and three follow-up mailings were used to solicit survey participation. The attitude survey questionnaire was composed of three parts: (1) demographic information on deaf leaders, (2) inquiries about their experiences with interpreters, and (3) the attitude statements about interpreters and interpreting. The respondents were asked questions within the scope of the three-part survey questionnaire as follows:

Part I: Demographic Information

Part I of the questionnaire includes demographic questions about deaf leaders' residency and their personal background related to gender, age, education, and holding offices such as a president, vice president, secretary, treasurer, or board member of the NAD and/or the State Associations of the Deaf for several or many years at some point between 1960 and 1999.

Part II: Deaf Leaders' Experiences with Interpreters

In Part II, survey respondents were asked to answer questions related to their experiences with interpreters. Questions focus on the leaders' frequency of interpreter use; involvement with current interpreting issues; negative experiences, such as lack of confidentiality, poor sign-to-voice interpreting skills, and poor judgment; interpreter complaint procedures; type of interpreter preference; access to interpreters; children of deaf adults (CODAs); and satisfaction with interpreters within the past two years. I also inquired if the leaders believe that CODAs are more skilled interpreters than those who are not CODAs (see Related Interpreting Questions on page 81–82).

Part III: Attitude Statements about Interpreters and Interpreting

Part III included the instrument composed of 12 attitude items. Eleven items were related to the attitude domain of interpreter competency, and one item was for monetary compensation. A Likert-like format allowed one of four possible responses to represent the respondent's degree of agreement or disagreement with each item: strongly agree (SA), agree (A), disagree (D), and strongly disagree (SD). Seven statements were worded in a positive direction; five were worded in a negative direction. After the survey, the five negatively worded attitude statements were reverse-coded.

There is no previously developed designation of attitude domains on which this study could be based. Therefore, this researcher identified eight attitude domains: interpreter certification, interpreter competency, interpreter education, hostile-dependency, monetary compensation, socialization, trust, and complaint procedures through a literature review of books, journals, and articles about interpreters and interpreting, as well as his professional involvement with interpreters. The content review and development of these domains and attitude items were based on interviews with professional interpreters, deaf people involved with interpreting issues, and college professors who had trained students in the field of interpreter education. After conducting two pilot studies, interpreter competency and monetary compensation were the two domains represented on the final version of the attitude scale.

RELIABILITY ANALYSIS

First, the distribution for each item was examined. Second, item-total correlations were calculated. The monetary compensation item was eliminated because it had poor correlations with the other items. Subsequently, the reliability analysis used items related to interpreter competency only. Measures of skewness and kurtosis were produced. Cronbach's alpha reliability statistic was calculated on the instrument. The reliability disclosed .6233 for alpha and .6367 for standardized item alpha. The reliability was at the lower limits of acceptability, but was acceptable for exploratory research.

POPULATION AND SAMPLE

As previously stated, the population for this study was defined as the past and present officers/board members of the NAD and the State Associations of the Deaf from 1960 to 1999. The NAD Home Office helped this researcher compile a list of the organization's officers and board members. The compilation of officer lists was based on the NAD membership roster, similar information from the State Associations of the Deaf, the *1999 TDI National Directory & Guide* published by the Telecommunications for the Deaf, Inc., and the *Alumni Directory* published by Gallaudet University. The NAD Home Office also tried to ensure that known deceased officers were not included. The final mailing list included the names and addresses of 1,655 officers/board members.

A target sample size of 160 leaders was established. This number was sufficient to conduct the statistical analyses. At a .05 significance level, assuming a small effect size and a power of .90, a sample size of 155 was required (Cohen & Cohen, 1983). Schroedel (1984) found that a typical response rate to mail surveys for people who are deaf or have other disabilities was between 25% and 30%. Therefore, using Schroedel's lowest rate (25%), the target sample size would be exceeded. To achieve the target sample size, 60% of 1,655 officers and board members were randomly selected to receive the letter of invitation to participate in the survey. The 60% random sample resulted in the invitation of 994 leaders (494 males and 500 females) to participate in the survey. Because multiple mailings were used on an issue of importance to the population, the target sample size was exceeded.

A total of 695 respondents sent back surveys. For the study sample, 502 respondents were qualified as deaf leaders because they were past or present officers/board members and a total of 193 respondents were not qualified. In addition, 56 surveys were returned due to wrong addresses. Two individuals died during the survey, and 241 people did not participate.

Delimitations

For this study, only leaders are included in the sample. It is difficult to conduct a random sample from the general deaf population. A representative sample of the leaders may differ from the general population in relation to their positions and knowledge about interpreting issues.

FINDINGS

In this section, findings from each of the three parts of this study will be described. Part I consists of a description of the demographic makeup of the respondents, Part II consists of a description of the respondents' experiences with interpreters, and Part III consists of a description of the results of the study of respondents' attitude statements about interpreters and interpreting.

PART I: DESCRIPTION OF THE SAMPLE

From Part I of the attitude survey questionnaire, the ensuing explanations of deaf leaders' demographic characteristics included residency, gender, age, education, and holding offices in NAD and the State Associations of the Deaf.

Respondents from 50 states and the District of Columbia participated in the survey. The largest number of respondents came from such populated states as Connecticut, Maryland, Massachusetts, New Jersey, New York, Ohio, Pennsylvania, Texas, and Virginia. Approximately 35% of the leaders lived in urban areas, 48% in suburban areas, and 17% in rural areas.

Two-hundred-seventeen leaders were male and 177 leaders were female. The age of the respondents ranged from 26 to 97 years of age. The mean age was 53.4 (SD = 13.29). In relation to the education of deaf leaders, 38 respondents had an A.A. or A.A.S. degree, 88 respondents had a B.A. or B.S. degree, 122 respondents had a M.A. or M.S. degree, and 17 respondents held a Ph.D., Ed.D. or J.D. degree. Overall, approximately 67% of respondents held a college degree, whereas approximately 33% did not (Table 1).

This information provides background information about the respondents to Parts II and III of this study. Part II, the attitude survey questionnaire, will be described in the next section.

PART II: DEAF LEADERS' EXPERIENCES WITH INTERPRETERS

In Part II of the attitude survey questionnaire, the leaders' experiences with interpreters included the respondent's frequency of use of interpreters, involvement with current interpreting issues and concerns, interpreter evaluation, bad or negative experiences, interpreter complaint procedures, type of interpreter preference, and satisfaction with interpreters within the past two years.

In the area of the respondent's frequency of use of interpreters, 107 respondents (27.9%) used an interpreter daily or several times a week, 131 respondents (34.2%) once a week or several times a month, and 145 respondents (37.9%) once a month or less than once a month.

When the respondents were asked about their current involvement with interpreting issues, 37.4% reported that they were involved. Of this group, 20.4% took active participation in the certification of interpreter candidates at the state or national level. Other ways the leaders were involved included serving on interpreter-related committees, which were sponsored by the State Associations of the Deaf, state chapters of RID, commissions or councils for the deaf and hard of hearing, and the interpreter quality assurance panels.

TABLE 1. *Demographic Information on Deaf Leaders*
(N = 394)

Demographics	*n*	Percent
Gender		
Male	217	55.1
Female	177	44.9
Age Range	26–97	
Mean Age	53.4	
Standard Deviation	13.29	
Education/Degrees Held		
Do not hold a degree	129	32.8
A.A. or A.A.S.	38	9.6
B.A. or B.S.	88	22.3
M.A. or M.S.	122	31.0
Ph.D., Ed.D., or J.D.	17	4.3

In relation to having bad or negative experiences with interpreters or interpreting, 216 respondents (54.8%) said, "yes," whereas 178 respondents (45.2%) answered that they did not have a negative experience. Those respondents having bad or negative experiences wrote the following specific reasons: time lag, late arrivals, patronizing, ego-control problems, lack of training, deficient American Sign Language (ASL) skills, poor reverse-interpreting (sign-to-voice) skills, poor attire, no facial expression, immaturity, explaining instead of interpreting, bad attitudes, using Signed Exact English (SEE) instead of ASL, exaggerated ASL and facial expression, and getting personally involved.

In the area of interpreter complaints, 102 respondents (25.9%) filed a complaint about interpreters, whereas 292 respondents (74.1%) did not file a complaint. Those respondents who filed a complaint explained in writing how they dealt with their complaints. Of 102 respondents, 56 expressed their satisfaction with the outcome and resolution of their complaints.

As for accessing an interpreter, 55% of the respondents made contacts with interpreter referral agencies when they needed an interpreter. Approximately 16% accessed interpreters by contacting either their workplace or local interpreter referral agencies. Approximately 8.5% used other methods, such as contacting an interpreter directly.

Approximately 54% of the leaders preferred those interpreters who used ASL, 40% chose those interpreters who used pidgin sign English (PSE), and 6% had a preference for those interpreters who used signed English.

PART III: DEAF LEADERS' ATTITUDES TOWARD SIGNED LANGUAGE INTERPRETERS

In the area of deaf leaders' attitudes toward sign language interpreters and interpreting, an analysis of data was based on the leaders' cumulative response to the mail survey. It involved one analysis of the attitude scale and its psychometric properties and a series of analyses based on the four research questions.

Comparisons of Respondents Who Fully Answered the Attitude Scale with Those Who Did Not

Five-hundred-two respondents returned the survey. However, 394 respondents answered all of the attitude statements in Part III, whereas 108 respondents missed at least one of the attitude statements. Therefore, 394 respondents had full attitude data while 108 respondents had incomplete attitude data. Before proceeding with the research questions, I investigated to see whether those who fully completed the attitude statements were similar to those who did not. I compared the two groups on the basis of gender, age, education, frequency of interpreter use, recent negative experiences with interpreters, and satisfaction with interpreters in the past two years (Table 2).

Statistical tests for group comparisons were conducted. When the two groups of leaders were compared on the basis of gender, the proportions of male leaders who completed the attitude scale did not statistically differ from the proportions of female leaders who completed it; both groups were of approximately equal proportions. Their differences were not statistically different: $p = .511$.

The two groups of deaf leaders were compared on the basis of their ages. Those leaders who completely answered the attitude statements were younger than those who did not. The groups were significantly different at the 0.002 level.

TABLE 2. *Frequencies and Percentages of Returned Surveys based on Deaf Leaders' Response to the Attitude Statements*

Total Returned Surveys (N = 502)	Respondents Who Completed the Attitude Statements (n =394)	Respondents Who Did Not Complete the Attitude Statements (n = 108)
Gender		
Male	217 (55.1%)	55 (50.9%)
Female	177 (44.9%)	53 (49.1%)
	missing = 0	missing = 0
Mean Age	53.40	58.04
	missing = 0	missing = 0
Education		
College Degree	Yes - 265 (67.3%)	Yes - 60 (55.6%)
	No - 129 (32.7%)	No - 48 (44.4%)
	missing = 0	missing = 0
Frequency of Use of Interpreters		
Daily or Several Times a Week	107 (27.9%)	18 (16.3%)
Once a Week or Several Times a Month	131 (34.2%)	29 (27.9%)
Once a Month or Less than a Month	145 (37.9%)	57 (54.8%)
	missing = 11	missing = 4
Negative Experiences	Yes - 216 (54.8%)	Yes - 41 (38%)
	No - 178 (45.2%)	No - 67 (62%)
	missing = 0	missing = 0
Satisfaction with Interpreters	Yes - 310 (83.8%)	Yes - 95 (96.9%)
	No - 60 (16.2%)	No - 3 (3.1%)
	missing = 24	missing = 10

Those leaders who held a college degree were more likely to answer all of the attitude statements than those without a college degree; they were significantly different at the 0.03 level.

In the area of frequency of use of interpreters, those leaders who fully completed the attitude scale tended to use an interpreter more frequently than those who partially answered the attitude scale. The difference between the two groups of leaders was significant at the 0.006 level.

Based on the incidence of bad or negative experiences with interpreters, those leaders who had a negative experience were more likely to fully complete the attitude scale. The difference between the two groups was significant at the 0.003 level.

A significantly higher proportion of respondents who were not satisfied with interpreters completed the attitude scale than those who were satisfied. The difference between the two groups was significant at the 0.001 level.

In summary, leaders who fully completed the attitude scale tended to be younger and more educated and to have a higher frequency of using interpreters with a greater degree of exposure to negative experiences than the leaders who missed one or more attitude statements. To conduct the analyses for the research questions, I used the data from those leaders who answered fully the attitude scale.

Analysis of Attitude Scale

Based on the respondents' completion of the attitude scale, the mean for the attitude scale was 26.7 (ranging from 11 to 44) with a standard deviation of 3.63. These data were distributed approximately normally (skewness = -.338, kurtosis = 1.069). High scores indicated that the attitudes of deaf leaders towards interpreters and interpreting tended to be positive, whereas those leaders with low scores were inclined to have more negative attitudes.

In order to understand the interrelationships among the primary variables, a correlation matrix was produced (Table 3). As can be seen, significant positive correlations were found between attitudes and age, attitudes and satisfaction with interpreters, age and satisfaction with interpreters, education and frequency of interpreter use, education and negative experiences, and frequency of interpreter use and negative experiences. Significant negative correlations were found between attitudes and education, attitudes and frequency of interpreter use, attitudes and negative experiences, age and education, age and frequency of interpreter use, age and negative experiences, and satisfaction with interpreters and negative experiences.

TABLE 3. *Bivariate Correlations among Primary Study Variables*
(N = 361)

Variable	1	2	3	4	5	6
1. Age	1.00					
2. Education Levels	-.259**	1.00				
3. Frequency of Use of Interpreters	-.372**	.359**	1.00			
4. Bad or Negative Experiences	-.242**	.198**	.330**	1.00		
5. Satisfaction with Interpreters	.106*	-.040	-.069	-.286**	1.00	
6. Attitudes	.199**	-.148**	.207**	.323**	.383**	1.00

Notes. $*p = .05$ $**p = .01$
Used listwise deletion (missing = 33)

Research Question #1: Do Attitudes Vary with the Age of Deaf Leaders?

The first analysis conducted used a hierarchical multiple regression. Age was entered first and frequency of use of interpreters second as independent variables. The attitude score was used as the dependent variable. Age accounted for 4.2% of the variance ($p= .0005$), whereas frequency of use of interpreters accounted for 2.2% of the variance ($p= .003$). Therefore, approximately 6.5% of the variance was accounted for by age and frequency of use of interpreters.

Research Question #2: Are Frequency of Interpreter Use and the Incidence of Negative Experiences with Interpreters Associated with the Leaders' Attitudes?

For the second analysis, two groups of the leaders were formed on the basis of whether or not they had a negative experience with an interpreter within the past two years. An analysis of covariance (ANCOVA) was used to examine the relation of the leaders' recent negative experiences with interpreters to their attitudes. The attitude score was the dependent variable, whereas negative experiences functioned as the independent variable. Age was used as the covariate because a preliminary analysis had shown age to be related to negative experiences with interpreters. Age was also related to the dependent variable. Of 394, 216 respondents (M = 25.675, SD = 3.486) had negative experiences, whereas 178 respondents (M = 28.039, SD = 3.368) did not have negative experiences. The ANCOVA revealed significant differences between leaders with recent negative experiences and those without recent negative experiences. Neither age (the covariate) nor the interaction of negative experiences with age was significant.

Research Question #3: Do the Views of Male Leaders and Those of Female Leaders Differ?

For comparing the attitudes of male and female leaders, the attitude score functioned as the dependent variable, whereas gender was the independent variable. Both groups of leaders had similar means and standard deviations. The mean for male leaders was 26.894 (SD = 3.589), whereas the mean for female leaders was 26.559 (SD = 3.672). The difference between the attitudes of male leaders and those of female leaders was not significant (p = .363).

Research Question #4: Does the Educational Level of Deaf Leaders Influence Their Attitudes?

The one-way ANOVA was used to see whether there were attitudinal differences among the leaders based on their education levels. Education levels ranged from "did not attend college"; to "attended college for one year, two years, or three years"; to "received an associate's, bachelor's, master's, or doctoral degree." Attitudes appeared to be related to the leaders' level of education. When ranking the means of attitude scores on the basis of education levels from the smallest to the largest, it did not follow the hierarchy of education levels. According to the post-hoc tests, the significance of the ANOVA was based on the difference between those leaders with a master's degree and those who did not attend college (Tukey, p = .019; Bonferroni, p = .026). No other post-hoc comparisons were statistically significant.

Summary of Research Question Results

To summarize the results on the basis of the research questions, the analyses for the first research question revealed that the attitudinal variance with the age of deaf leaders was significant, and frequency of use of interpreters and negative experiences were associated significantly with the leaders' attitudes. Furthermore, age and frequency of use of interpreters influenced attitudes because their total variance in attitude scores accounted for approximately 6.5%. Therefore, the influence of the two variables was statistically significant, but their combined influence was small. The third research question included an analysis about the difference between the views of male and female leaders, but the attitudinal difference based on gender was not significant. The fourth research question demonstrated that education was significant. In addition, the multiple comparison analyses using Tukey and Bonferroni disclosed that those leaders with a master's degree and those who did not attend college were statistically different, whereas those with other education levels were not statistically different.

Supplementary Analysis

The earlier hierarchical multiple regression with age and frequency of use of interpreters accounted for a small part of variance in attitude scores. The ANCOVA results showed the relationship between negative experiences and attitudes. Therefore, supplementary analyses were run to see whether negative experiences would add to the variance accounted for. Additionally, this researcher noted that reported satisfaction with interpreters was related to the attitude score. For the first supplementary analysis, a t test was used to compare those who were satisfied with those who were not. The t test results were significant. Twenty-four of the 394 respondents did not answer the question about satisfaction with interpreters in the second part of the attitude survey.

Because the results from the satisfaction analysis were significant, two more steps were added to the hierarchical multiple regression to see how much variance was accounted for by negative experiences and satisfaction. Age was entered first, followed by frequency of use of interpreters (as in the original analysis for the first research question), with negative experiences entered in the third step. With this three-variable model, the total variance in attitude scores accounted for was approximately 13%.

TABLE 4. *Supplementary Hierarchical Multiple Regression Analysis Explaining Variance in Deaf Leaders' Attitudes Based on Age, Frequency of Use of Interpreters, Negative Experiences, and Satisfaction with Interpreters (N = 361)*

	Multiple R	R+	Adjusted R+	R+ Change	F Change
Age	.199	.039	.037	.039	14.754*
Frequency of Use of Interpreters	.245	.060	.055	.020	7.790*
Negative Experiences	.353	.125	.117	.065	26.467*
Satisfaction	.465	.216	.207	.091	41.328*

Note. *p = .0005

Negative experiences added 6.5% of the variance in attitude scores. Therefore, negative experiences accounted for approximately the same amount of variance as age and frequency of use of interpreters combined. In the fourth step, satisfaction accounted for approximately 9% of the variance in attitude scores, bringing the total variance accounted for to approximately 21% (Table 4). Thirty-three of the 394 respondents did not answer the questions about frequency of use of interpreters and satisfaction with interpreters.

Analyses with the Larger Sample

As noted earlier, the respondents who fully answered the attitude scale differed from those who partially answered the scale on several variables. Therefore, the question arises: Would the results differ if the incomplete respondents could be included? Therefore, I identified those respondents who skipped only one of the 11 items on the attitude scale. Of the 108 respondents who did not complete the attitude scale, 59 skipped only one item. By using a mean substitution procedure, I included those 59 respondents in the sample. I re-ran the major analyses for the research questions using this larger sample (*n* = 453). Comparing the results of the original analyses with these analyses revealed that the results were essentially identical to the original analyses. That is, statistically significant findings from the original analyses were statistically significant with the larger sample. Nonsignificant results remained non-significant.

CONCLUSION

The "Interpreter Training—the State of Art" conference in 1979 reported that there was little knowledge about attitudes toward sign language interpreters and interpreting, and there was no previous data to assess the attitudes of deaf people (Gallaudet University, 1979). Since the late 1980s, NAD and RID have addressed the issue of deaf people's dissatisfaction with interpreters to resolve interpreter-related problems and concerns through NCI. This study collected data from a select group of deaf people, specifically national and state leaders, concerning their attitudes and characteristics that might influence these attitudes.

The study had two parts: (1) developing the attitude scale and (2) investigating the relationship of attitudes to the selected characteristics of deaf leaders. The first part related to the measure of attitudes of deaf leaders, and the second part explored what characteristics of deaf leaders would relate to their measured attitudes about interpreters and interpreting.

Prior to the distribution of the mail survey, I finalized the attitude scale, which was composed of 12 statements in a Likert-like format based on 11 interpreter competency items and one monetary compensation item. The reliability necessitated the removal of the monetary compensation item because it correlated poorly with the other items. Accordingly, the attitude score was based on the sum of the 11 interpreter competency items. The reliability, though low, was acceptable for exploratory research.

The sample was majority male (55%). The mean age was 53.4 years. Educational levels were quite high, with approximately two-thirds of the leaders holding a college degree or better. Almost 55% of the leaders confirmed that they had negative experiences with interpreters. Nonetheless, approximately 84% of the leaders were satisfied with the interpreters they had used within the past two years.

Age, education, frequency of use of interpreters, negative experiences, and satisfaction with interpreters within the past two years were characteristics of deaf leaders that were related to attitudes. Attitudinal differences based on gender were not found. Age, education, and frequency of use of interpreters were considered as personal characteristics of the leaders, and negative experiences and satisfaction with interpreters were seen as experiential characteristics because they were related directly to the interpreting interaction.

The combined influence of age and frequency of use of interpreters on attitudes was statistically significant when they accounted for approximately 6.5% of the variance in attitude scores, a significant but relatively small portion of the variance. When I conducted supplementary analyses using negative experiences and satisfaction with interpreters, these two variables accounted for approximately 15% of the variance in attitude scores, more than twice the variance in attitude scores accounted for by age and frequency of use of interpreters. Education levels and attitudes did not demonstrate a linear relationship; the post-hoc tests revealed that the difference between those leaders with a master's degree and those leaders who did not attend college was significant.

LIMITATIONS OF THE STUDY

Even though the results of this study revealed some interesting patterns, the study does have several limitations. The attitude scale had a minimally acceptable reliability for exploratory research. Low reliability means that there is more error in measurement. Therefore, relationships among variables may be reduced or not found. The validity of the attitude scale was not tested, but the study provided some support for validity. Those leaders who reported having negative experiences had significantly lower attitude scores than those without negative experiences. Those leaders who reported being satisfied with their interpreters had scores that were significantly higher than unsatisfied leaders. Clearly more work is needed on the reliability and validity of the attitude instrument.

I used a randomly selected sample of deaf leaders, but approximately 22% did not fully complete the attitude scale. When those respondents who completed the attitude scale and those who did not complete the attitude scale were compared, there were significant differences based on age, education, frequency of use of interpreters, negative experiences, and satisfaction with interpreters. Gender was not significant. Therefore, the analyzed sample may not be representative of deaf leaders in general. However, by examining the data of these leaders who did not fully complete the attitude scale, I was able to add approximately one-half of them to the sample. The analyses based on the larger sample showed that the results did not change.

RECOMMENDATIONS FOR FUTURE RESEARCH

Although a growing body of research that addresses deaf consumers' perspectives about interpreters (Livingston, Singer, & Abrahamson, 1994; Stauffer and Viera, 2000) and consumers' expectations or schema regarding interpreted interaction (Metzger, 1995; 1999) is available, this is the first study that has measured deaf leaders' attitudes about interpreters and interpreting. Though this research has revealed some interesting results, it touches on a number of issues and concerns that need further investigation.

Further study about the general deaf population and its views about interpreters and interpreting are needed because the average deaf person's attitudes may be different from the leaders' general attitudes. The sample of leaders was certainly not representative of the general deaf population. Because approximately 67% of the leaders had a college degree, they are more educated than the general deaf population. Moores (2001) noted that not many deaf students completed four-year educational programs to receive a bachelor's degree; only one-third of deaf post-secondary students had the intent to pursue the degree, and only 5% actually received it. Average deaf people are not, in general, inclined to become intimately involved with interpreting issues. They simply use interpreters as needed to conduct necessary transactions with hearing people.

This researcher's measure of attitudes was a measure of general attitudes. The data related to what the leaders thought about interpreters and interpreting was based on their cumulative experiences with interpreters. However, recent research has begun to focus on signed language interpreting which occurs in specific situations. For example, Roy (1989; 2000) studies an interpreter participating in a meeting between a deaf graduate student and a university professor; Metzger (1995; 1999) and Sanheim (2003) examine an interpreted pediatric encounter with a hearing doctor, deaf mother, and hearing child; and Richey (2003) analyzes aspects of interaction in an interpreted sermon. Interpreting situations can vary from platform interpreting for a lecture or discussion panel to mental health interpreting to phone interpreting. These situations will tend to vary in their significance for a deaf person. For example, if a deaf person is attending a public lecture and the interpreter is doing a terrible job, the deaf person might feel upset or angry, but his or her life is not really affected. However, if he or she is in a doctor's office or counseling session and the interpreter is doing a bad job, this situation could have serious effects. The first interpreting situation does not carry the trust and confidentiality issues that the second situation does. Therefore, attitudes about interpreters and interpreting may vary by the type of interpreting situation because different interpreting situations tend to emphasize particular aspects and issues of the interpreting process.

Situation-specific attitudes relate to the individuals' feelings about interpreters and interpreting in more narrow contexts. In this regard, interpreting in sensitive contexts such as doctor's appointments, counseling appointments, job interviews, courtrooms, parent-teacher conferences, and so forth may tend to highlight particular aspects of the interpreting process. For example, in the area of mental health interpreting situations, Stewart et al. (1998) stated that deaf people may tend to show a reluctance to use an interpreter when they seek counseling because they may hesitate to expose socially unacceptable behaviors such as substance abuse or martial infidelity before interpreters they know in the community. Research related to characteristics of specific interpreting situations is needed to identify which characteristics are most salient to that situation and how they relate to attitudes.

Future research should include the deaf person's preference regarding situation-specific social factors such as the gender and/or age of interpreters in a medical encounter with a doctor or surgeon or the mental health counseling environment. Deaf people's trust in the interpreter's ability to maintain confidentiality in the area of situation-specific attitudes needs further study because attitudes related to highly personal or sensitive interpreting situations may vary from general attitudes.

The psychometric properties of the attitude measure should be improved. Interpreter competency items that were represented on the attitude scale can also be improved. Though the item-total correlations were acceptable, inter-item correlations for several items were low (below .10). These items will need to be revised to improve their contribution to the attitude scale. Additionally, new items reflecting other competency areas should be added. Examples of competency areas could include ASL grammar use, appropriate sign selections, and appropriate use of body positioning. Those competency items were not included on my scale.

Finally, future research should also address consumer preferences and attitudes as they relate to language contact. Lucas and Valli (1992) and Bayley, Lucas, and Wulf (2000) provide a detailed description of variation in sign use resulting from contact between deaf and hearing communities. Since Winston's seminal study of transliteration in 1989, a growing body of studies related to the process and products of translit-eration and how it compares with interpreting have been published (see, for example, Livingston, Singer, and Abrahamson [1994]; Sofinski et al. [2001]; Sofinski [2003]; and Winston and Monikowski [2003]). Consumer attitudes about language choices in interpreted encounters could also relate to trust and confidence in an interpreter's linguistic abilities or to any of the factors addressed in this study.

Recommendations for future research about interpreters and interpret-ing include the need for future study related to attitudes of the general deaf population, the need for improvement in the psychometric properties of the attitude measure for the attitude scale of interpreter competency items, and further research related to general attitudes and situation-specific attitudes, including the issues of trust, confidentiality, and sensi-tivity.

To increase awareness of deaf people's attitudes toward interpreters and interpreting, future study should include research related to improv-ing the measurement of attitudes, improving knowledge about the char-acteristics of deaf people, and developing a scale related to the interactive interpreting process. Research should include different types of interpreting situations in order to study general attitudes and situation-specific atti-tudes. Roy (2000) suggests that the need exists for research related to in-terpretation in many arenas as well as the need for using diverse methodologies. Future research in this and the aforementioned areas could go a long way toward informing not only consumers and practitioners of signed language interpretation, but also the field of interpretation and trans-lation at large. Such studies would also be useful in studies of sociolinguistics in general and improving the understanding of language attitudes and language policy and planning. These studies would also inform scholars and educators in the areas of deaf studies and interpretation.

REFERENCES

Bayley, R., Lucas, C., & Rose, M. (2000). Variation in American Sign Language: The case of DEAF. *Journal of Sociolinguistics* 4 (1), 81–107.

Cohen, J., & Cohen, P. (1983). *Applied multiple regression/correlation analysis for the behavioral sciences* (2d ed.). Hillsdale, NJ: Erlbaum.

Gallaudet University (1979). *Interpreter training—The state of art*. Washington, DC: Author.

Gannon, J. R. (1981). *Deaf heritage—A narrative history of deaf America*. Silver Spring, MD: National Association of the Deaf.

Livingston, S., Singer, B., & Abrahamson, T. (1994). Effectiveness compared: ASL interpretation vs. transliteration. *Sign Language Studies* 23 (82), 1–54.

Lucas, C., & Valli, C. (1992). *Language contact in the American deaf community*. New York: Academic Press.

Metzger, M. (1995). Constructed dialogue and constructed action in American Sign Language. In C. Lucas, (Ed.), *Sociolinguistics in deaf communities*. Sociolinguistics in Deaf Communities vol., 1. Washington, DC: Gallaudet University Press.

Metzger, M. (1999). *Sign Language interpreting: Deconstructing the myth of neutrality*. Washington, DC: Gallaudet University Press.

Moores, D. F. (2001). *Educating the deaf—Psychology, principles and practices.*Boston: Houghton Mifflin.

National Association of the Deaf. (1986). *National Association of the Deaf convention proceedings at Salt Lake City, Utah*. Silver Spring, MD: Author.

Nettles, C. (1996). Development of joint interpreter test planned. *The NAD Broadcaster, 18* (7 & 8), 8–9.

Richey, M. A. (2003). Analysis of interactive discourse in an interpreted deaf revival service: Question-answer adjacency pairs initiated in an ASL sermon. In M. Metzger, S. Collins, V. Dively, & R. Shaw (Eds.), *From topic boundaries to omission. New research on interpretation*. Studies in Interpretation, vol. 1. Washington, DC: Gallaudet University Press.

Roy, C. (1989). Features of discourse in an American Sign Language lecture. In C. Lucas (Ed.), *The sociolinguistics of the deaf community*. San Diego: Academic Press.

Roy, C. (Ed.). (2000). *Innovative practices for teaching sign language interpreters*. Washington, DC: Gallaudet University Press.

Sanheim, L. M. (2003). Turn exchange in an interpreted medical encounter. In M. Metzger, S. Collins, V. Dively, & R. Shaw (Eds.), *From topic boundaries to omission. New research on interpretation*. Studies in Interpretation, vol. 1. Washington, DC: Gallaudet University Press.

Schein, J. D. (1981). *A rose for tomorrow: Biography of Frederick C. Schreiber.* Silver Spring, MD: National Association of the Deaf.

Schroedel, J. C. (1984). Analyzing surveys on deaf adults: Implications for survey research on persons with disabilities. *Social Science & Medicine* *19* (6), 619–627.

Sofinski, B., Yesbeck, N., Gerhold, S., & Bach-Hansen, M. (2001). Features of voice-to-sign transliteration by educational interpreters. *Journal of Interpretation,* 47–68.

Sofinski, B. (2003). Adverbials, constructed dialogue, and use of space, oh my! Nonmanual elements used in sign language transliteration. In M. Metzger, S. Collins, V. Dively, & R. Shaw (Eds.), *From topic boundaries to omission: New research on interpretation.* Studies in Interpretation, vol. 1. Washington, DC: Gallaudet University Press.

Stauffer, L. K. & Viera, J. (2000). Transliteration: A comparison of consumer needs and transliterator preparation and practice. *Journal of Interpretation,* 61–82.

Stewart, D. A., Schein, J. D., & Cartwright, B. E. (1998). *Sign language interpreting—Exploring its art and science.* Boston: Allyn and Bacon.

Winston, E. (1989). Transliteration: What's the message? In C. Lucas (Ed.), *The sociolinguistics of the deaf community.* San Diego: Academic Press.

Winston, E. & Monikowski, C. (2003). Marking topic boundaries in signed interpretation and transliteration. In M. Metzger, S. Collins, V. Dively, & R. Shaw (Eds.), *From topic boundaries to omission. New research on interpretation.* Studies in Interpretation, vol. 1. Washington, DC: Gallaudet University Press.

Part II **Practice**

What Are You Suggesting?

Interpreting Innuendo Between ASL and English

Shaun Tray

Interpretation of innuendo is a complicated undertaking. This is true for monolingual users of a language, but even more so for professionals who are interpreting live and interactive discourse. To gain a better understanding of effective strategies for interpreting innuendo, one must first understand innuendo and its form and function in both languages involved. To study innuendo, one must investigate numerous components of language that make up, or function as, innuendo. Chief among those are humor and indirectness. To understand a speaker's intent, an addressee must have reached a level of communicative competence to recognize the speaker's contextualization cues. Both the cues and the competence to recognize them are culturally bound. Therefore an interpreter working interlingually and cross-culturally must have the appropriate level of competence in each language. Even so, systemic problems related to the use of innuendo within interpreted encounters may affect the outcome. In order to gain a better understanding of the ways in which interpreters convey innuendo in American Sign Language (ASL)-English interpreted interaction, this study addresses both the conveyance of innuendo by native Deaf signers of ASL and the interpretation of innuendo from English into ASL. For this study, two Deaf actors performed an English script in ASL, and two interpreters interpreted an audio version of the script into ASL. The script is fraught with innuendo. The performances and interpretations were analyzed to determine the strategies used to convey the humor and insinuation by native signers of ASL and ASL-English interpreters.

LITERATURE REVIEW

Defining Innuendo

By its most pedestrian definition, *innuendo* is a hint or sly, usually derogatory, remark or an insinuation.[1] Conversationally, it may be represented by zingers, sarcasm, witticisms, double entendre, and similar wordplay like verbal parody, irony, and understatement. For this paper, *innuendo* is defined as utterances that carry an implicit derogatory meaning aimed at a particular target, often guised with humorous intent or faux naiveté. What most of the contemporary research calls *punning* would comply with this definition of innuendo. Punning, however, is an insufficient label because it fails to capture the same conversational impact created by ellipses, ambiguity, and allusions. For interpreters, this broad definition allows for a variety of communicative events that pose similar challenges to the task of conveying a message from the source language (SL) to the target language (TL). Foremost of those challenges is the issue of form versus meaning. It is a characteristic of languages that one form may express numerous meanings, and one meaning may be expressed through numerous forms (Larson, 1998). For interpreters, figurative use of language presents a potential difficulty because they must determine the speaker's intent for choosing the nonprimary meaning.

Just as many variations of wordplay humor have been gathered under the umbrella heading of innuendo, so too have variations in indirect communication. This runs contrary to other research on indirectness. In a study about indirectness in political discourse, for example, Obeng (1997) defines specific categories of verbal indirectness, such as evasion, innuendo, circumlocution, and metaphor. Each category explains a distinct kind of verbal misdirection or a particular discourse strategy. Innuendo in that study is narrowly defined as an insinuation about an interactant's character. Circumlocution is based on Goffman's work and is defined as "a variety of evasive tactics deployed by an interactant to protect himself or herself against face-fall" (Obeng, 1997, p. 55). Obeng specifically differentiates between circumlocution and innuendo, saying, "Unlike other verbal indirectness strategies such as metaphor, innuendo, proverbs, and aphorisms which exploit the polysemy of words, circumlocution pertains to the rhetorical structure of discourse" (ibid, p. 55).

For this paper, however, both the innuendo and circumlocution categories above will constitute innuendo. Certainly Obeng's definition of innuendo falls directly into the scope of the term's definition for this paper. Circumlocution will be included because humor and indirectness are two typical evasive tactics used by interactants to save face. Goffman's definition deftly describes one of the primary functions of innuendo in conversation. This will be discussed in greater depth later in this paper. Still, Obeng's distinction of circumlocution does underscore the breadth of innuendo, which is not only reflected in lexical or phrasal items, but may also be characteristic of a discourse-level strategy.

Linguistics, it seems, finds this umbrella category of innuendo too all-encompassing for sufficient analysis. To investigate the relevant aspects of innuendo, one must consider applicable research on puns, jokes/humor, indirectness, figurative language, irony, and parody. Information for this literature review was gathered from fields of linguistics, sociolinguistics, pragmatics, sociology, ethnography of communication, semantics, psychology, and anthropology. This paper cannot capture all the information available, but it will highlight particular findings from researchers that interpreters use to develop strategies to address innuendo.

Humor and Innuendo

Humor research has approached the topic from two perspectives: appreciation and production. The emphasis in linguistics fields has been primarily on the former, leaving most of the latter to psychology. Production of linguistics humor has received almost no attention from researchers (Pepicello & Weisberg, 1983). Some reasons for this will be outlined in the Issues with Research to Date portion below. Research conducted on humor appreciation has historically focused on jokes and puns. These forms of humor lend themselves naturally to analysis because the rituals involved offset them from other parts of a conversation. Phrases like, "Did you hear the one about . . . ?" or "Two guys walk into a bar . . ." mark the utterance to follow as a joke. Similar kinds of phrases have been found for puns and riddles. Analysis, then, is bound by the introduction and the punch line. This allows researchers to follow tried-and-true methodologies used to study other clearly bounded communication like greetings and leave-taking. Puns are similarly offset from the rest of the sentence and easily studied as a comparison between the true word and the pun.

Sociolinguistics changed the complexion of how communication is studied by investigating conversation in context. Researchers recognized that people do not speak in complete sentences. Attention was turned from studying sentences to studying utterances—the less-bound fragments of sentences that people use to communicate. So too has the focus broadened in humor research as investigators seek to learn more about nonbounded humor used in conversational joking. Herein lies the opportunity to discover more about innuendo, which, as mentioned above, is intertwined with verbal irony, teasing, conversational punning, and the like. Moreover, observing in context how innuendo is used can provide some insight into the speaker's goal when he or she chooses that discourse strategy.

Innuendo is a deliberate speech act that capitalizes on the context of the moment. Rosen-Knill and Henry (1997) outline four essential acts for verbal parody that can be minimally adapted to provide an outline of innuendo (Table 1). Understanding the innuendo requires the addressee to recognize the speaker's intent, appreciate the performance of the utterance, understand the derogatory meaning, and appreciate the humorous tone. Without each step, the speech event falls short.

It is not the aim of this study to delve into Freudian explanations of humor motivation. Still, issues of conversational joking inherently address interactant behaviors as demonstrated by turn-taking, face-saving and face-threatening acts, and general conversational control issues. These harken back to theories of humor as a form of aggression. Given the derogatory aspect of innuendo reflected in the critical act above, one should particularly expect such connections. At the same time, humor is often credited for creating a bond between the interactants. The age-old advice to public speakers is open with a good joke. Saville-Troike (1998) points out, "Joking is also a common way of mitigating criticism that might not be acceptable if given directly" (p. 34). Throughout this paper, the paradox of humorous innuendo as simultaneously face-threatening and face-saving will be discussed, as will the similar contradiction that it is disruptive and cohesive in intent.

Indirectness and Innuendo

Every definition of innuendo includes a reference to its indirect nature. Questions immediately arise as to how the subsequent indirect meaning is recognized by the addressee and what purpose it serves for the speaker.

TABLE 1. *Outline of Innuendo*

Verbal Parody	Innuendo
1. The intentional representation of the object of parody toward a target	1. The deliberate insinuation
2. The flaunting of the verbal representation	2. The flaunting of the implication
3. The critical act	3. The critical act
4. The comic act	4. The comic act

First, how is indirectness understood by the addressee when the speaker uses a figurative meaning? According to Saville-Troike (1998), "situated meaning must be accounted for as an emergent and dynamic process" (p. 22). To describe this process, Gumperz (1977) uses the term *conversational inference*. Conversational inference is highly context-bound. Participants in a conversation use it to interpret one another's intentions, interpret meaning, and build the conversation. Using verbal and nonverbal responses, each participant acknowledges his or her understanding of what is being said. Both Saville-Troike and Gumperz discuss the importance of perceiving the salient features of the linguistic message and integrating that with extralinguistic cultural knowledge. In this way, the meaning is negotiated by the interactants.

Searle (1975) discusses the role of illocutionary force in indirect speech acts. Suffice it to say, a speaker can produce an utterance that has a meaning different from what he or she actually says. "There are also cases in which a speaker may utter a sentence and mean what he says and also mean another illocution with a different propositional content" (ibid, p. 59). As an example, he explains that *Can you reach the salt?* is not merely a question but a request to pass the salt. While under the right circumstances that may be an actual question of one's physical ability, most often it is a recognized idiomatic request. In a case of dialogue, Searle analyzes the following sentences:

Student X: Let's go to the movies tonight.
Student Y: I have to study for an exam.

Most people would recognize Y's response as declining X's proposal, but the literal meaning is simply a statement of fact about Y—seemingly unrelated to the first utterance. To explain how X determines that Y is rejecting the offer, Searle details a 10-step process that integrates facts from the conversation, principles of conversational cooperation, speech act theory, factual background information, and inferences that X would utilize. Of course interactants do not consciously go through these steps. They occur naturally during the dialogue as a part of Gumperz's conversational inference and Saville-Troike's dynamic process. Searle's steps do, however, reveal the opportunities for innuendo in indirect communication. One must simply suspend the principles of conversational cooperation at that point in the process. While this explanation of how the meaning of innuendo is understood by the addressee only scratches the surface, it does provide enough foundation to move forward.

The Role of Innuendo in Conversation

With an understanding of what elements of communication constitute innuendo and how they are recognized, the appropriate next step is to discover what purpose innuendo serves in a conversation. Within any given situation, under what circumstances will a speaker choose innuendo as a discourse strategy—and to achieve what end? Obviously, the generalized functions of humor and indirect communication mentioned above can be applied to innuendo. A more thorough insight can be gained, however, from research conducted on four of those functions: inclusion, exclusion, subversion, and circumlocution. In each case, innuendo serves as a strategic tool for communication.

Inclusion

The inclusive function of innuendo as humor is demonstrated in two circumstances: (1) between strangers and (2) within a community. When people meet for the first time, often they feel a need to "break the ice" (i.e., move past the initial uncomfortable feeling to build rapport). In a review of the sociology literature on the study of humor, Fine (1983) discusses research on how men use sexual humor in bars to gauge a woman's reaction for additional contact. If the woman rejects the joke, the man can save face by asserting that his true invitation was not rejected, only the joke. If the woman laughs, the man assumes she is open to more intimate contact. The humor, then, is not merely a vehicle to initiate conversation, but a device to insinuate the speaker's true intention. Separate from questions about the methodology of humor research, it is easy to recognize that innuendo can be used early in relationships to imply expectations.

Humor is also used to build a community. Fine highlights research about the Chippewa Indians that found "one of their categories of humor is humor that promotes group solidarity. . . . This humor is directed internally through testing, mutual ribbing, good fellowship, and even humorous self-deprecation" (173). The result is a trusting, communal relationship. This philosophy often motivates the rituals of initiations in a variety of social organizations. Community-building can also be demonstrated by gallows humor. Fine explains this phenomenon as humor that grows out of situations wherein an oppressed group pokes fun at its oppressors. The humor is often bitter and is used to galvanize the oppressed by transforming their plight into a source for unity. This gallows humor can function as subversion.

Exclusion

It seems logical that if humor can function as a device for inclusion that it can serve similarly as a device for exclusion. They differ, of course, only in one's perspective of the situation. For example, a Deaf joke may unify the community with a punch line that emphasizes the us-against-them mentality of gallows humor, in which members of the Deaf community triumph over the majority non-Deaf society. It is inclusive for Deaf people and exclusive from the non-Deaf perspective. Similarly a Deaf joke may target a Deaf individual who has, in the opinion of the group, strayed from accepted group norms. The humor again reinforces the communal identity and implicitly threatens the target with exclusion from the group for the violation. In this way, it controls the target's behavior. Sociologists label inclusion and exclusion as social conflict function and social control function, respectively (Fine 1983).

Subversion

Carried to an extreme, both social conflict and social control humor begin to function as subversion. The speaker can "foster demoralization and social disintegration of the group [control], or induce a hostile attitude toward an out-group [conflict]" (ibid, p. 174). At this level of aggression, the feigned guise of humor serves as an attempt to deflect retaliation from the target. Fine mentions numerous studies into black/white humor, Czech/Nazi humor, and Arab/Israeli humor as examples. Left unchecked, the attitudes that the humor inspires can proliferate. The former Soviet Union recognized the power of subversive humor and often jailed those who challenged the authority of the state with jokes. The defense for the accused, then, was essentially, "What? You can't take a joke?!"

Circumlocution

Whereas the first three roles of innuendo relate to its humorous aspects, the final role, circumlocution, relates to the indirect nature of innuendo. Obeng (1997) analyzed how politicians speak and determined that indirectness is essential for communicating difficult messages—those that threaten face. For those in a political arena, saving face is tantamount to saving one's career. Given the heterogeneity of addressees in an audience for any given utterance, politicians often use innuendo to avoid potentially damaging communication.

Finally, the last motivation for using innuendo to be addressed here is that often times innuendo is the most accurate expression. "The indirectness itself will contribute to the contents of the concept and make it altogether different from a directly expressed concept" (Geukens, 1978, p. 266). For a detailed account comparing addressees' reaction to indirectness, see Colston and O'Brien (2000) and Leggitt and Gibbs (2000) for their work on verbal irony.

Linguistics of Humor

As mentioned above, appreciation of linguistic humor has been researched for many years. This section will feature those aspects of the research applicable to interaction. After an overview of the mechanics of humor, this section will address how the use of conversational joking impacts communication from a sociolinguistic perspective.

Notice in Table 2 how different fields describe humor in their research. This list is by no means meant to suggest homogeneity within the fields; instead it is a reference tool, a summary of general information. Reading down the center column, it becomes clear that each of the fields attributes a kind of duplicity (frame shifting and script overlap) or disingenuousness (incongruity and discontinuity) to humor. Goffman (1974, p. 11) defines frames as "definitions of a situation [that] are built up in accordance with principles of organization which govern events—at least

TABLE 2. *Descriptions of Humor by Discipline*

Discipline	Description	Author
Sociology	Frame shifting	Goffman
	Discontinuity or bisociation	Fine
Contextual Semantics	Script overlap & Incongruity	Raskin
Semantics	Incongruity-Resolution	Pepicello & Weisberg
Cognitive Psychology	Incongruity Resolution	Suls

social ones—and our subjective involvement in them." An activity like a business meeting may be framed as a professional event, but a humorous remark from a participant reframes the activity to one of play. Other participants must recognize the change in frames to understand the humor.

This reframing is what other researchers call incongruity or discontinuity. Essentially, play is not compatible with a professional business meeting. Another example, a comment to a coworker that he is looking couth, kempt, and sheveled is humorous only after the addressee realizes that the speaker has exploited bound morphemes, that is, the compliments are not actually English words (Pepicello & Weisberg, 1983). That is an incongruity. Suls (1983) even compares humor appreciation to problem-solving skills. He posits that humor requires (1) a "play" cue, (2) extreme divergence, and (3) an appropriate time scale to comprehend the humor. Suls' Incongruity Resolution Model (Figure 1) outlines the steps to appreciate humor.

The logical next question is how does the addressee recognize a "play" cue? According to Gumperz (1977, p. 199), "It is the process by which we evaluate message meaning and sequencing patterns in relation to aspects of the surface structure of the message, called 'contextualization cues.'" The addressee uses the cues to determine the signaling of interpretative frames. These may include paralinguistic and intonation contours, but Gumperz emphasizes that contexualization cues are highly culturally specific. This concurs with other research that interpreting the meaning of an utterance requires communicative competence (Hymes, 1974) and the ability to understand the speaker's meaning (Grice, 1975). Communicative competence is "a system of its [language] use, regarding persons, places, purposes, and other modes of communication, etc.—all

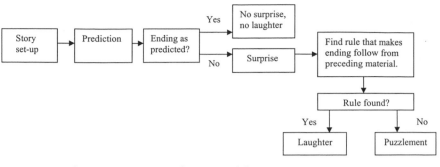

FIGURE 1. *Suls' Incongruity Resolution Model*

the components of a communicative event, together with attitudes and beliefs regarding them" (ibid, p. 75). Communicative competence is acquired in tandem with other aspects of language acquisition. Table 3 summarizes this information. Taken in total, one can see that "meaning in conversations is usually jointly produced" (Gumperz, 1977, p. 195). No participant wholly controls the meaning of an utterance himself.

Grice (1975) developed the Cooperative Principle for conversations and its four maxims:

- **Quantity.** Give exactly as much informative as required.
- **Quality.** Say only what you believe to be true.
- **Relation.** Be relevant.
- **Manner.** Be succinct. (ibid, p. 45)

These outline the goals for the speaker and conversely the expectations for the addressee. The addressee will follow these maxims to determine the speaker's meaning. This becomes critical for understanding humor, and particularly innuendo, in that the incongruity, discontinuity, etc., seemingly violates Gricean maxims. Raskin (1985), however, found a way to reconcile the Gricean maxims with humor by adapting them as non-bona fide communication: Raskin's application of maxims for non-bona fide communication (joking):

- **Quantity.** Give exactly as much informative as is necessary for the joke.
- **Quality.** Say only what is compatible with the world of the joke.
- **Relation.** Say only what is relevant to the joke.
- **Manner.** Tell the joke efficiently. (ibid, p. 103)

TABLE 3. *Focus for Understanding Innuendo*

Discipline	Focus	Author
Anthropology	Contextualization Cues	Gumperz
Ethnography of Communication	Communicative Competence	Hymes
Pragmatics	Speaker's Meaning	Grice

Grice asserts that in the spirit of conversational cooperation, the addressee will make every effort to treat sentences that violate the maxims as nondeviant to the greatest extent possible. Once the utterance can no longer be considered bona fide communication, however, he will look for humorous context (Raskin, 1985). This sequenced search for meaning complements the frame shifting theories discussed above. The sequence triggers the innuendo as the addressee recognizes the incongruity of the utterance, cannot reconcile it within Gricean maxims, discovers a match in Raskin's adapted maxims, and finally comprehends how the speaker shifted frames.

An example of this process is the remark, "at band camp," uttered as an aside by a student in a graduate-level interpreting class. The remark is succinct, but violates each of the other three Gricean maxims: In a feedback discussion of ASL to English interpreting, it is certainly not relevant, and it does not provide enough information for an addressee to determine the veracity of the statement. Yet, because the utterance satisfied the maxims for non-bona fide communication, the addressee immediately recognized it as an allusion. The utterance completed a catchphrase from the movie *American Pie*. In context of the class, the speaker noticed a mannerism in the target, as he frequently used the phrase, "This one time . . .," in his interpretation. By simply completing the catchphrase, the speaker used the real-life classroom context to create and resolve an incongruity and carried with it the impact of the movie character who originally spoke the line. Out of context, most people would not recognize, much less appreciate the humor, but the speaker and addressee managed to negotiate meaning from the utterance.

With an overview of how humor and innuendo are recognized, it is important to investigate the impact they have on a conversation. Norrick (1994) points out the contradictions mentioned above, that conversational joking is associated with both aggression and rapport. It is disruptive and yet can intensify cohesion. "If the attempt at humor is understood and accepted, participants in the conversation may enjoy enhanced rapport; but if hearers do not get the joke or feel joking is inappropriate in the current context, the result can be misunderstanding, disruption of involvement, and loss of rapport" (ibid, p. 411). Norrick explains that conversational joking is disruptive because it forces hearers to "disregard contextually obvious meanings and look for obscure interpretations outside the current topic and activity" (p. 411). He also points out that humor is volatile in that certain kinds of humor will be accepted in one setting but not another.

Fine (1983) made the same assessment regarding the participants involved. "Joking is a strategic activity. By that I mean that not everyone can joke about all topics in all situations" (p. 165). A contemporary example comes from an episode of *Seinfeld*. Jerry complains about another comedian who starts using Jewish material in his routine just after converting to Judaism. "I think he just converted for the jokes!" Seinfeld cries. The implication relates to the discussion above about inclusion and exclusion. Seinfeld contends that the comic has not been Jewish long enough to be considered a part of the community. He is still an outsider; therefore, the humor is offensive. Fine cites sociological studies that revealed humor is judged funnier when it disparages groups other than that of the addressee or holds the addressee's group in esteem. Therefore, a Jewish joke told at a Jewish event will in all likelihood be regarded as a disruption if told by a non-Jew, but as an opportunity to increase rapport if told by a member of the community.

Norrick (1994) uncovers another paradox of conversational joking. Using punning as an example, he explains that humor is aggressive not only to the subject (target), but to the addressee as well. Because puns are usually not prefaced the way other jokes are, the humor is a pop quiz of sorts. By putting the addressee on the spot, the pun is aggressive. At the same time, punning "provides a way of talking off record, so that we can manipulate the flow of topics, test for shared background knowledge and attitudes, and realign participants in non-confrontational ways" (p. 415).

Much of the research and many of the examples in the paper deal generically with humor. The issues presented all apply to innuendo, but there are risks unique to this genre as well. The most obvious is the ability to disclaim a joke. A traditional joke is marked, and if the addressee rejects it, the speaker can shrug it off to some degree, saying, "It's not my joke. It's not like I wrote it or anything." Innuendo is contextual and self-generated. In an article on conversational joking and identity display, Boxer and Cortes-Conde (1997) discuss the high risk involved in such an encounter. Their study on teasing showed that the encounters occurred between intimates and were meant to enhance the existing bond. Given the delicate nature of the speech act, however, the speaker could go too far.

Remember that meaning is negotiated between speaker and addressee. That allows for misinterpretations or faux misinterpretations that will affect the result. Zajdman (1995) listed possible outcomes of face-threatening acts (Table 4). It clearly shows that despite the speaker's intent, the possibility exists that the utterance will not be received accordingly. Leggitt and Gibbs (2000) recognized the negotiation involved in their study of verbal irony. "Verbal irony critically depends on the desire to communicate intentions that do not directly match the words, and the correct interpretation of ironic language depends on recognizing that disparate intention" (p. 5). Tannen (1986) uses a baseball analogy to capture the spirit of exchanges like innuendo. "The speaker feels clever for having pitched a curve ball, the hearer for having caught it. But if the curve is not caught—if it hits someone in the head or flies out of the ball park—no one is happy" (p. 62).

One way for the speaker to avoid these pitfalls is to mark the innuendo, but that has consequences of its own. Some studies have investigated how the speaker might set off the utterance. Boxer and Cortes-Conde (1997) refer to studies wherein the speakers use disclaimers or exaggerated intonation, laughs, or winks to mark the utterance. Barbe (1993) analyzed explicit irony in written English. She selected Letters to the Editor that contained phrases like "it is ironic that . . . ," "ironically . . . ," and "in a rather ironic twist of fate . . ." from two newspapers. What is striking is Barbe's observation in the footnote about the selection of these sources: "It is interesting, and perhaps worth investigating, that professional writers of satires seem to avoid the explicit use of irony" (p. 582). Of course they do. Irony, innuendo, etc., are indirect by nature. Explicating irony by calling it such or following innuendo with the tag "if you know what I mean," undermines the intent of the form. It is a linguistic rim shot. The speaker avoids being taken literally, but as a conversation style, the technique leaves him looking like the stereotype of a bad stand-up act, "Hey, these are the jokes, folks." One need only look to the Monty Python sketch in which the character follows up each utterance with a

TABLE 4. *Possible Outcomes of Face-Threatening Acts*

Speaker's Intention	Hearer's Interpretation	Speaker's Expectation	Hearer's Expectation
Meaning offense	Taking offense	Insult	Insult
Meaning offense	Not taking offense	Insult	Amusement
Not meaning offense	Taking offense	Amusement	Insult
Not meaning offense	Not taking offense	Amusement	Amusement

vocalized stream of markers—"wink, wink, nudge, nudge, say no more, very good then"—to see the backlash of revealing the implication.

Issues with Research to Date

As mentioned earlier, linguistic research into humor has focused on appreciation rather than production. One of the great barriers, especially for the study of conversational joking, is naturalness. Experimenters in all fields try to strike the perfect balance between naturalness and control. Spontaneity is a key feature of conversational joking. The example above, "at band camp," was hysterical in context and not the least bit amusing outside of it. One might appreciate the depth of wit required to create the humor, but it does not have the impact without the spontaneity. Some studies have focused on control by using written English (Barbe, 1993; Leggitt & Gibbs, 2000); others chose to record actual interactions to analyze (Boxer & Cortes-Conde, 1997; Hay, 2000). Logistics must be considered either way. For example, would the subjects in the Leggitt and Gibbs study react differently to the verbal irony if they saw it in context and heard the intonation rather than reading it from a page. Hay mentioned in her own background material that men and women use humor differently. Men tend to perform while women tend to use it cohesively. The subjects did not know Hay was analyzing humor, but they did know they were being recorded. Does that make the speech event a performance and potentially inhibit the speakers? Hay, like all researchers of natural human interaction, is constrained by Labov's Observer's Paradox (1972). By simply being involved, personally or via electronics, the researcher changes the dynamic.

Still, these studies are a great deal more sensitive to factors that contribute to humor than some prior research. For example, Hay points out that much of the research to date has been conducted by men, naturally from a male-centric perspective. That has led to misconceptions that women do not have a sense of humor or can't tell jokes, and even speculation that women are not aggressive enough to tell jokes. In one example mentioned in Fine (1983), a study was conducted on men in bars to see how they use and respond to humor. It revealed that men tend to laugh more at risqué jokes when they are told by beautiful women than when they are told by unattractive women. The obvious problems with this study are: 1) Who decided the jokes were funny to begin with? and 2) Who decided how attractive the women were? Beyond the mental image of a formal Request for Participants advertising for ugly women to tell dirty jokes, readers of these investigations must be particularly attentive to the researchers' methodologies.

Indirectness in American Sign Language (ASL)

While the breadth and depth of ASL research is ever increasing, the fact remains that the field itself is not yet even four decades old. Innuendo, as defined for this paper, is only now beginning to be investigated in English discourse after centuries of linguistic research; it should not come as a surprise then that research into even the broadest related issues of ASL is sparse. Since the earliest work of Stokoe (1960), which inspired decades of linguistic research into ASL as a natural human language, only one published study has analyzed the structural and grammatical possibilities of wit and punning (Klima & Bellugi, 1979). Considering that humor has only been a viable topic for investigation in linguistics roughly as long as ASL has been recognized, limited research demonstrating that witticisms and "plays on signs" do indeed exist in the language may not be surprising.

Unfortunately, the minority status of ASL users coupled with the nonaural and unwritten modalities of the language has allowed many assumptions about ASL and the American Deaf community to fill the void of research yet to be conducted. Consider the long-held notion that Deaf people are blunt (Lane, Hoffmeister, & Bahan, 1996, p. 73). Such an assumption would lead one to believe that it is impossible to use innuendo when indirect communication is not commonplace. Roush (1999) challenged the stereotype of the blunt Deaf person when he brought indirectness strategies in ASL to light. Although indirectness in general goes beyond the scope of this paper, several of Roush's points are key to an understanding of the possibility of innuendo in ASL.

Roush acknowledges the stereotype of directness in Deaf people and emphasizes that it is as strong inside the Deaf community as it is with those outside the community who interact with its members. Typically, issues related to changes in the addressee's physical appearance, speaker disclosures, and advice are cited as examples of that directness. The rationale is that directness facilitates communication and promotes solidarity through sincerity. Roush posits, however, that these goals are tempered by strategies for independence and saving face.

While he notes that more research must be done on indirectness in ASL, Roush does mention several examples that are commonplace. Criticism may be offered in an indirect manner with phrases that translate roughly to "this is not the Deaf way" to emphasize a sense of community; bilingual Deaf people may also appropriate more English-like politeness strategies to convey indirectness; and ASL also makes use of euphemisms such as:

> GONE for deceased
> BROTHER/SISTER for gay or lesbian, respectively
> MONTHLY for menstrual period
> (Roush, 1999, p. 36)

In addition to lexical substitution for taboo topics, signs may be altered to reduce their visibility for the sake of subtlety. For example, *menstrual period* may be conveyed with a particular nonhanded sign made at the location where the standard ASL sign is produced.

Roush's research is the foundation for analysis of the role of innuendo in ASL. First, he has demonstrated that ASL has strategies and use for indirect communication. Second, the examples of euphemisms for taboo topics parallels topics that are often discussed figuratively in English as well. This bodes well for the probability of innuendo, which also tends to capitalize on taboo topics. Moreover, the shared background of taboo topics (death, sexuality, sexual orientation, bodily functions) may also bode well for interpreting innuendo on those topics cross-culturally. Future research should investigate the ethnographic role of innuendo in ASL and Deaf culture. If ASL does indeed have innuendo, what function does it serve? Does innuendo in ASL parallel innuendo in English as euphemisms seemingly do? Answers to these questions lead in turn to development of strategies for interpreting innuendo between the two languages.

ASL Sign Play

While it has not yet been proven linguistically whether ASL makes use of innuendo, or what function innuendo might serve, anecdotal evidence reveals that ASL does indeed have figurative uses that satisfy the definition of innuendo for this paper. Deaf entertainer Elmer Priester was known in the 1940s for his performance of an adult version of "Yankee Doodle Dandy." According to Padden and Humphries (1988), "[the performance] suggests that he knew at least enough about the language to be able to select signs that subtly suggested another meaning, yet were similar enough to the original song so people would recognize the joke" (84). Beyond this anecdotal example and research by Roush, little has been developed regarding indirectness in ASL. ASL morphology, however, has been the subject of much study.

A great deal of research has focused on ASL morphology. (For overviews, see Baker-Shenk & Cokely, 1980; Valli & Lucas, 1992.) Rather than discuss morphology in general, this paper will highlight some aspects of morphology used to create a "play on signs." Using the patterns of words or signs that already exist, languages can create totally new forms (Valli & Lucas, 1992, p. 51). Deaf poet Eric Malzkuhn demonstrated his ability to manipulate ASL morphemes when he prepared and performed his translation of "Jabberwocky." Just as Carroll had created fantastical words from combinations of known English words in the original, Malzkuhn combined recognized morphemes from standard ASL signs to bring the mystical characters to life (Padden & Humphries, 1988). This recognition of language structure and the ability to manipulate the components are the basis for puns, which themselves may be used for innuendo.

As discussed above, puns and jokes have received the lion's share of researcher's attention relative to other forms of wordplay categorized as innuendo in this paper. Again, this is because they tend to be self-contained utterances, which are more easily analyzed. The same is true in the only published research on ASL wit. Klima and Bellugi (1979) investigated the poetic function of ASL; half of their paper focused on manipulating signs for punning. To be clear, at this time, their was no deliberate attention paid to the function of punning from a sociological or ethnographic perspective, but rather a much more basic question about whether puns were even possible in ASL. "Perhaps, or so this question sometimes implies, the existence or non-existence of the special form of wit known as punning could give us clues to the status of ASL as a language, since punning relies so heavily on the form of a language" (ibid, p. 106). Even so, some of the data was gathered in what amounts essentially to ethnographic interviews. These led the researchers to the conclusion that not only does punning exist in ASL, but that it functions as wit in communication.

Klima and Bellugi outline three processes for creating puns in ASL:

- Process 1: Overlapping two signs simultaneously or holding part of one sign as another sign is produced.
- Process 2: Blending two signs into one complex unit.
- Process 3: Phonological manipulation, which is substituting one prime for another in one of the four sign parameters: handshape, location, palm orientation, and movement.

An example of overlapping (not from Klima and Bellugi) roughly translates into English as "book smart, but no common sense." The pun is created by overlapping the sign for KNOWLEDGEABLE (C-handshape at the forehead) and STUPID (2-handshape). The 2-handshape for the pun is placed in front of the KNOWLEDGEABLE sign rather than directly on the forehead. The blending in process 2 can be clearly seen in the name sign for former President Richard Nixon. Klima and Bellugi explain the pun is developed by blending the sign for LIE with the bound morpheme N, the initial for the former president's last name. The third process includes many puns that are becoming lexicalized, such as THINK-HEARING and GOOD-QUESTION (QUESTION made with 4-handshape).[2] MJ Bienvenu (personal communication, 2000) pointed out that such puns are often accepted as standard ASL by nonnative signers who do not recognize them as plays on signs.

According to Bienvenu, true punning (as opposed to those becoming lexicalized) may be used conversationally as humor for its own sake or indirect communication like a veiled insult. To illustrate her point, she used the example ?INTERPRET—the standard sign INTERPRET produced with hands crossed at the wrist and nonaffected facial expression. When discussing the lack of skill of an interpreter, one might choose direct utterances with predicate adjectives like

INTERPRET^AGENT LOUSY (or INEPT).

Another approach would be the use of nonmanual adverbs, as in

__th_____

PRO.3 INTERPRET

Certainly, an explanation could serve the same purpose. For example,

PRO.3 INTERPRET. WRONG++ AWFUL. CAN'T UNDERSTAND PRO.3.

Choosing to use the pun,

PRO.3 ?INTERPRET

is indirect. The signer relies on the addressee's communicative competence and shared background of interpreting services to arrive at the implied message. In this way, the pun seems to function as innuendo.

The puns THINK-HEARING and ?INTERPRET also uncover another potential similarity to how innuendo is used in English. In English, innuendo is often used to mask aggression. Roush focused his research to prove that a frank language did in fact have indirectness strategies, so puns that function as veiled insults were beyond the scope of his work. A logical next step for future research then is the ethnographic function of negative indirectness in ASL. If similarities are found between English and ASL uses of negative punning, strategies could be developed to benefit interpreters working with that language pair.

HYPOTHESIS

Given the anecdotal evidence of innuendo in ASL from Padden and Humphries (1988) and research confirming punning and indirectness in the language (Klima & Bellugi, 1980; Roush, 1999, respectively), it seems possible that an English message fraught with innuendo can be effectively interpreted into ASL. The question then is: What form best conveys the intended message? Remember, the heart of innuendo is the insinuation—what is actually left unsaid. "The unsaid is consistently present in humor whose base is language. Mainly, humorists make use of their audience's unstated expectations" (Dolitsky, 1983, p. 41). That means the interpreter must decide which information can or must be included to achieve the same implication in the target language. Further, he must consider if the target language utterance will produce the intended humor cross-culturally. If the innuendo is based on a pun or the polysemy of an English word, one would expect the interpretation to reflect the necessary changes to the message in order to signal ASL users of the humor and/or ambiguity.

For this project, an English script was performed in ASL by Deaf actresses. The same script was interpreted from an audiotape by artistic interpreters. I hypothesized that the analysis would reveal differences between the two groups. The actresses, whose native language is ASL, would have a different understanding of a Deaf audience's unstated expectations. Moreover, I anticipated the actresses' ASL utterance to reflect greater communicative competence through the use of different contextualization cues than those of the interpreters whose native language is English. It is not the intent of this project to evaluate the dramatic or interpreting skills of the participants overall, rather it is to uncover similarities and distinctions in the strategies employed to convey the English-based humor in ASL.

METHODOLOGY

Four participants were recruited for this project: two actresses and two interpreters. All the participants were female to constrain one possible variable in the outcome. Research has found that men and women use humor differently in conversation (Tannen, 1990; Hay, 2000). While no research was found on how men and women differ in the performance of humor, it seemed appropriate to control for the variable nonetheless. Table 5 summarizes the fundamental information.

Table 5's category "Years of Experience" shows how many years of experience each person has in their chosen area: acting or interpreting. The questionnaire asked for years experience in each category, but neither actress reported any interpreting experience or training, nor did either interpreter list any theatrical experience or training. Both interpreters are certified CI and CT through the Registry of Interpreters for the Deaf. All participants are Caucasian and are students at Gallaudet University.

Each participant was given a script in written English; the interpreters also received an audiotaped script. *The Princess Plays with Wood* was selected as the source text because of its extensive use of innuendo and the punch line that depended on the building implications. Additionally, the risqué humor would make it clear if the message was understood. An audience might laugh or might be offended, but one way or another, they would recognize the incongruity within the script. *The Princess Plays with Wood* is a three-character skit set on a news interview program. Miss Linda is a renowned children's book author who is being accused of hiding sexual images in her texts. Rod P. Longacre is the program's host who manages the attack and rebuttal exchanges between Miss Linda and

TABLE 5. *Characteristics of the Actresses and Interpreters*

Characteristics	Actress A	Actress B	Interpreter A	Interpreter B
Native Language	ASL	ASL	English	English
Age	19	19	36	27
Years of Experience	4	11	12	6
Education	In college	In college	In grad school	In grad school

her challenger. The humor arises as the challenger reads excerpts from the book that contain sexual overtones, and the author rationalizes them away.

The original script made use of a variety of humorous techniques. In order to focus the participants on the innuendo, the script was edited (Appendix A). In addition to emphasizing innuendo, the abridged version had only two characters rather than the three in the original. The neutral character (the host in the original) was eliminated. The host then took over the antagonist role to challenge Miss Linda directly on behalf of his viewers. In the end, Miss Linda convinces Rod that her books are indeed innocent, and the stage is set for the punch line. Reducing the cast was done to make the script less complicated with characters to juggle, since each participant would perform the scene alone.

The scripts were highlighted to show the participants the innuendo. The goal was not to see if they could recognize the humor; it was to see how they would convey it. Just as with a real theatrical performance that would have a director, sign master, and/or dramaturge, the participants were permitted to use additional resources. I functioned as the director when necessary to explain the overall tone of the script, but did not get involved in how the lines were interpreted or delivered. The participants were not permitted to prepare the material together. The participants had seven days to prepare. After each participant was filmed, she was given a short questionnaire (Appendix B) to gather demographic information and her opinions about the material, the results, and her effectiveness.

The rating scale went from 3 to 0. An even number of choices was deliberately offered to avoid having the participants settle for the middle answer. The numbers will not be computed in some pseudo-statistical analysis, rather they will be used to evaluate the questions on a greater than/less than basis. For example, both interpreters rated the difficulty of the interpretation higher than their satisfaction with the results. In this way, the numbers can offer some insight into the participants' thought processes.

Inside the Numbers

Both interpreters and one actress rated the English script a 2 or 3 (very funny). Actress A rated it a 0 (not funny at all). The same three rated the ASL version of the story lower than the English script, with Interpreter B showing the largest disparity (3 and 1, respectively). Again, Actress A differed from the others, rating the ASL version a 3. As mentioned above, both interpreters rated the difficulty of the interpretation higher than their satisfaction with the results. Actress A rated the difficulty and her satisfaction equally (2), and only Actress B rated the difficulty lower than her satisfaction (1 and 2, respectively). Table 6 summarizes the information.

Notice that Interpreter A rated the ASL material a 1.5. That answer was accepted because it satisfied the goal to show relativity. Although the participants were given the material days in advance to prepare, the three who completed the comments portion of the questionnaire indicated that more time would have improved their presentations. Actress A made no comments.

These numbers uncover two points for comparison. First, three of the four participants judged the material funnier in the source language (SL) than the target language (TL), which indicates that they recognized the script was designed to exploit specific SL features. How then could Actress A, who was not amused by the script in the least, manage to create a performance that topped the scale? The details become clear in the observations below, but generally the numbers reveal the participants' decisions about form versus meaning. Actress A seemingly did not appreciate the SL form and instead focused solely on the meaning to perform the ASL version. The other three participants acknowledged the humor in the English form and attempted to convey it more specifically as part of the meaning in the TL performances.

The second comparison follows the actress–interpreter divide. Why is the difficulty to satisfaction ratio neutral or positive for each actress, but negative for both interpreters? Each actress and Interpreter A evaluated her effort as a 2 (favorable). But Actress B found the task relatively easy (rating it a 1), while Interpreter A judged the task very difficult (3) to

TABLE 6. *Actress and Interpreter Ratings of Material*

Questions about the material	Actress A	Actress B	Interpreter A	Interpreter B
Did you find this material humorous in English?	0	3	2	3
Did you find this material humorous in ASL?	3	2	1.5	1
How difficult was this interpretation/ performance?	2	1	3	2
Are you satisfied with your efforts?	2	2	2	1

Scale: (Very) 3   2   1   0 (Not at all)

achieve the same level of satisfaction. As noted above, both of these participants decided to convey the SL form as a part of the meaning in the ASL performance. I hypothesized that the Deaf participants, whose native language is ASL, would demonstrate greater communicative competence in the TL. Certainly these numbers do not quantify the communicative competence, but they do seem to reflect the participants' own assessment of the effort required to demonstrate that competence.

Actress A did not find the material as easy to perform as Actress B did. Consider though that from her estimation, she was working with inadequate material (rating the script a 0). The task required more effort, but produced comparable satisfaction. Interpreter B was not satisfied with the results of her efforts. That naturally produced a negative ratio. A possible specific explanation for the disparity in the difficulty to satisfaction ratio between the actresses and interpreters is discussed below.

Observations from the Videos

The script sets up the innuendo in the story by presenting two frames. On the surface, the children's book author, Miss Linda, has written a charming little story about a Princess building bookshelves for her Prince. The second frame was the Princess' affair with Big Bob the carpenter. In English, the humor capitalized on turns of phrase like "Big Bob had a really big tool and knew how to use it, the Princess could screw like no one else in the kingdom," and even the title of the book itself, *The Princess Plays With Wood* to manipulate the audience's focus. Each phrase contains a double entendre:

- Tool = tool or penis
- Screw = a screw or the act of intercourse
- Wood = wood or an erect penis

Other innuendo came from ambiguity, as in the line, "As the Princess watched the carpenter do it . . ." The context is deliberately vague to allow the audience to determine what "do it" refers to. The scripted dialogue is a series of accusations and rebuttals between the interviewer and Miss Linda. The interviewer finds an excerpt from the book that suggests the Princess is having an affair with the carpenter, and the author explains it away. The exchanges are written to be humorous themselves and to set up the punch line to close the story.

The actresses and interpreters utilized many similar strategies to convey elements of the innuendo, and these will be discussed below. First, it is important to understand how the participants set up the frames initially. This is key because the two groups established the frames differently. In ASL, each participant set the stage for the duplicity of events with a challenge from the interviewer:

Script: Now, some people feel your books are a bad influence on our children. They claim your books are full of sexual innuendo and blatant erotic content that can easily damage children's innocent minds.

Actress A: [the book] PEOPLE FEEL FULL S-E-X-U-A-L E-R-O-T-I-C

Actress B: SOME PEOPLE GOSSIP BAD INFLUENCE CHILDREN BECAUSE WOW (gesturing indecision) S-E-X EXCITE IN BOOK VERY BAD

rhq

Interp A: BOOK #N-G FOR CHILDREN. RUIN POSS.3 MIND HOW VAGUE S-E-X. OBVIOUS NOT. THINK RUIN POSS.3 MIND.

Interp B: PEOPLE COMMENT POSS.2 BOOK S-E-X MEANING BEHIND. SEE E-R-O-T-I-C. CHILDREN INNOCENT READ MIND CONFUSE SHOCK.

Both actresses make statements of fact (i.e., direct accusations of sexuality in the books). Notice that both interpreters, in contrast, immediately seize upon the implication in the story. Interpreter A says, VAGUE S-E-X.

OBVIOUS NOT, and Interpreter B says, S-E-X MEANING BEHIND. Both emphasize the word *innuendo* from the English script. In English, it forewarns the audience of the nature of the material yet to come. It foreshadows the second frame. The audience now has a heightened sense for the double meanings and waits in anticipation. The interpreters, whose native language is English, recognize the SL foreshadowing and establish the frames in the TL in kind. It is important to understand that neither interpreter merely passed through the information. Neither chose fingerspelling *innuendo* as an option to attempt setting the second frame. Each processed the English word and rendered an interpretation in grammatical ASL. Had the actresses used a similar process, the question of contextualization cues might not be raised. But the actresses used another technique.

The actresses set up the second frame in the next set of utterances. According to the script, "the Princess told her Prince, 'I'm going shopping', but really she was going to meet Big Bob the carpenter." In this section, both actresses used the sign SNEAK in lieu of GO to describe the Princess' intention to rendezvous with Big Bob. That lexical choice stands out to the audience. Certainly ASL has a verb to state the action "to go." In fact, both actresses used GO in the utterance before when the Princess announce that she was going shopping. The verb SNEAK certainly has an implied meaning of deception. With that insinuation, the second frame is created. The audience is looking for reasons why the Princess is sneaking. Interpreter B also took advantage of this part of the script for an implication. She used a direct address question, PRO.3 TRUE^WORK GO SHOP ("Did she really go shopping?"), just after the role shift in which the Princess said she was going shopping. Certainly the follow-up question to the audience undermines the veracity of the Princess' words.

Once the frames were established, the actresses and interpreters used various strategies to maintain them. Actress A relied on exaggerated signs to introduce doubt or create suspicion. As the interviewer, she used utterances like LOOK^LIKE INNOCENT with emphatic prosody that showed the speaker actually questioned the statement. Then she used CHANGE-PERSPECTIVE and OBVIOUS to underscore the presumption that something more than the surface meaning was happening.

Actress B used numerous other techniques to allude to the sexual references. More than any of the others, Actress B embodied the characters. That created opportunities for sly gestures like hair tosses, winks, and knowing expressions that served as contextualization cues. Like both interpreters, Actress B used an unnamed classifier with sexual overtones for Big Bob's tool.[3] The grammatical rule in ASL is to name the object before using a classifier to represent it—much like rules in English that govern pronoun use. As in English, suspending that rule with vague indexing allows the audience to make assumptions based on incomplete information. The assumed meaning is reinforced by the production of the classifier just below the established sign space. Moments later in the dialogue, the classifier is named a large hammer, but the audience has already intuited the sexual meaning based on the previous context.

A later excerpt from the children's story reads, "The Princess was quite handy in her own right. She could screw like no on else in the kingdom." The appalled interviewer reiterates, "That's right, 'she could *screw* like no one else in the kingdom!" Actress B and Interpreter B both use fingerspelling to convey SCREW. Interpreter B does not elaborate whether the topic is hardware or intercourse. She leaves it to the audience to decide which meaning of screw is intended, but does not mark the utterance in any way (coy expression, wink, etc.) that might suggest duality for the audience. Actress B uses the role shift as the interviewer to explicate the meaning:

```
_____rhq_
PRINCESS EXPERT WHOA WHAT EXPERT S-C-R-E-W SAME NONE OTHER.
MEAN PRINCESS EXPERT
```

```
_____ q _____
FUCK+++ BETTER THAN #ALL
```

Then she shifts to the author to calmly deny and downplay the insinuation with the other definition of the word *screw*. For the same exchange, Interpreter A used another unnamed classifier predicate with handshapes, expressions, and gestures that are typical when describing explicit sexual activities. The scene created a double meaning from which the audience could see sexual activity or manual labor.

Each of the participants exploited the blame and deny format of dialogue. As mentioned in the literature review, the participants negotiate the meaning in a conversation. In this skit, the actresses and interpreters negotiate the meaning via a dialogue between the characters, and the audience is a bystander who gains amusement watching the meaning emerge. In the four videos, the audience was addressed twice. In both cases, the direct address was used to draw the audience in and elicit a reaction. Breaking from the rhythm of the dialogue, Interpreter B became a narrator to question, PRO.3 TRUE^WORK GO SHOP. That technique forces the audience to consider the event. Was the Princess really going shopping? Actress B used a direct address that was less offset but even more straightforward. After a role shift in which the author proclaims the innocence of the passage, Actress B slides into the interviewer role, gives the camera a sideways glance, and signs:

— q —

TWO-OF-THEM FUCK. KNOW^THAT. (emphatic nod)

She then completes the shift to the interviewer. The entire exchange from the beginning of the author's denial to nod confirming, "of course you KNOW^THAT" takes less than three seconds, and most of that is body language and facial expression. She struck me as a Jerry Springer-like talk show host turning to the audience and saying, "You know he's putting it to her!" Comments like that are used to incite the audience. Because it is so brazen amidst the rhythmic give and take of the previous conversation, the audience inevitably reacts. Still, because the comment is outside the ongoing conversation, it does not give away the duplicity that the characters are creating.

The final decision for the participants was the punch line. Throughout the dialogue, they developed the incongruity. They created the innocent bookshelf-building frame and the illicit affair frame; to close, they would have to reconcile them. What actually transpired between the Princess and Big Bob? All but Actress B chose a matter-of-fact delivery. The children's book author reads the last line from her story in a sing-song, nursery rhyme manner.

> And in the wonderful kingdom of goodness and light, the fairies danced and the wood nymphs sang. The Prince admired his beautiful bookshelves and the Princess fucked Big Bob.

Both interpreters and Actress A matched that same affect with fluttery, flowing sign style and innocent expressions. Actress B chose a more expansive delivery with a less-than-thrilled reaction from the Prince about his gift and a dramatic pause before the last line. The pause is followed by an emphatic exclamation of the punch line and a final role shift to become the interviewer. Her facial expressions and body language say, "See, I knew it!" The accusations were true all along. Of the four performances, Actress B explicated the most information, but also convoluted the situation by exploiting the blame-and-deny format.

DISCUSSION

Limitations of This Project

This project introduces the issue of conveying innuendo interlingually and cross-culturally. Determining conclusive results from this particular study alone, however, should be done judiciously. Several factors could sway interpretation of the results (e.g., size of the study, disparity in participants, and level of participant involvement). These caveats should not deter other researchers and interpreters from considering particular aspects of the study. A great deal of information is available. One need only remember that this project is merely an introduction to the topic. Additional research is necessary to confirm and expand these findings.

First, a larger study might reveal more about the consistency of how interpreters and Deaf performers create and manipulate frames for the sake of humor and insinuation. With only four participants, the chances for coincidence are high. Moreover, a more diverse participant group might provide insight into gender, ethnic, and/or generational differences. Second, the experience level of the two groups is skewed. Both interpreters are certified professional freelance interpreters. They each have experience interpreting performing arts. The actresses are both undergraduate students majoring in theater. Problems potentially arise with the comparison of professionals to students. Lastly, the participants were recruited for this project. A faculty member from the Theater Department at Gallaudet University recommended the actresses, and several interpreters referred me to their colleagues with artistic interpreting experience. Each was asked to volunteer her time to prepare the performance. Although the script was short, the participants had to prioritize the preparation against classes, studies, and work.

Another consideration is that the performance was recorded without an audience. Recording and analyzing an actual performance and an interpretation of an actual performance with an audience present might have made the experience more natural for the participants. While the ASL performances might be more natural, however, that approach has more logistical problems. Researchers have studied such factors as the physical environment of comedy clubs on humor and the introductions of comedy performers by the emcees for building audience expectations. Beyond issues such as these is the critical consideration of each audience member's language background. These details quickly grew unmanageable for the primary objective of this study; the study intended to analyze the participants' strategies, not their performance skills, per se.

Implications for Interpreters

Researchers have investigated various types of figurative language individually. This project defined a wide range of this figurative language collectively as innuendo because they share pragmatic functions relative to humor and indirectness. These functions are problematic for interpreters on the job. Innuendo pervades everyday settings where interpreters work. While the source (script) for this project is arguably excessive, most interpreters can relate to communicative events like these:

1. *Without Bob how can we get anything done today?*
   - at a staff meeting

2. *A: Hurry up.*
   B: I'm coming . . . be there when I'm finished.
   - between colleagues

3. *A: You hear about Bill?*
   B: Yeah. Not that there's anything wrong with that.
   - between colleagues

Each example contains elements of indirectness and humor that function to achieve specific ends. Each is also a high-risk, face-threatening communication event. Consider the possible meanings inferred.

In utterance (1), the speaker interjects an opinion about Bob's absence that day. Without an understanding of the dynamics of that office, the statement might be literal—Bob is vital. On the other hand, Bob might be chronically absent or just lazy, and the statement is actually ironic. The exchange in (2) contains a pun, much like the kind of humor from the *Princess* script. The term *coming* might express either hurrying or climaxing. In this case, Speaker A's reaction to the pun will determine whether the humor builds rapport between the speakers or creates friction. Notice that in (3), the information about Bill is never stated. Instead Speaker B acknowledges comprehension of the question with an allusion to a *Seinfeld* episode.[4] These situations can be difficult for interpreters because of equivalence challenges and interactive issues.

The literature on interpreting abounds with perspectives regarding equivalence. The interpreter's goal is to convey an equivalent message from the SL to the TL. The crux of the argument stems from the issue of form versus meaning, particularly when the form is actually part of the meaning of an utterance. Such is the case for innuendo. Because the implication and/or humor of the utterance results from a play on words, linguistic ambiguity, or cultural reference, the form absolutely contributes to the meaning. In this way, it is like poetry and other figurative language use. This paper will not restate the range of ideas on this topic; instead see Larson (1998) and Frishberg (1990) for overviews. The intent of this section is to emphasize that even the fundamental premise of equivalence that strategies for interpreting innuendo can be built upon, are not uniform. Still, while the participants in this project used a variety of similar strategies to convey the innuendo, this study revealed uniformity between the contextualization cues used by the Deaf participants to trigger the frame shift, which was distinct from the interpreter's uniform approach to that task.

Humor depends on rules. "Humor gains its liberating power when the breaking of the rules is local and temporary" (Zajdman, 1995, p. 328). Again, the *rules* of conversation have been outlined above on the basis of Gumperz, Hymes, and Grice. Norrick (1994) labeled conversational joking as disruptive and jarring to these rules; still, as illustrated by Raskin's maxims for non-bona fide communication, even this disruption has a structure. Interpreters must know the rules and the acceptable ways to manipulate or break them in both the SL and TL to successfully produce innuendo in the TL.

One potential problem for ASL-English interpreters is the lack of formal education available in American Sign Language. Even native bilingual ASL-English interpreters do not have the access to the same opportunities for advanced education (perhaps even formal education of any kind) in ASL the way other interpreters have when each language in their language pair is regarded as a majority language. This is an obvious disadvantage when striving for equivalence in the message. While it may be argued that humor is rarely the point of language study, only those fluent in a language can expect to effectively manipulate its intricacies. Coupling that with the fact that many ASL-English interpreters are *not* native ASL users underscores the need for advanced language study.

Consider, for example, the most fundamental part of humor—creating the frames. In this project, the interpreters and actresses set up the frames with different tactics. The interpreters emphasized the innuendo as it would be done in English (i.e., the SL). The actresses used key lexical choices in the TL instead. The question arises then whether the audience would perceive all the information that follows the creation of the frames as equivalent to the script for each participant.

Psychology researcher Colston (2002) investigated how the receiver comprehends figurative language. He determined that contrast, predictability, and involvement are fundamental elements of understanding. In example (1) above, the greater the contrast between Bob's actual work performance (frame 1) and the comment about it (frame 2), the more humorous the comment will seem. The contrast must be predictable, which is to say that the receiver must be able to reconcile the two frames. Otherwise the utterance will be received as peculiar. Lastly, the more involved the receivers are in the situation, the more humorous they will find the comment. These are substantial hurdles to equivalence for an interpreter to overcome.

An interpreter who is not routinely involved with this group may not have any perspective on Bob's work habits, which limits any contrast. Perhaps based on the speaker's vocal prosody or the reaction of the other participants, the interpreter could observe that a frame shift occurred, which would allow for reaction, but would still fall short of prediction. Additionally, because the interpreter is not involved with the group regularly, he or she will receive the comment as less humorous. In total, that limited level of comprehension of the SL causes difficulty in reformulating a TL message with similar duality. Remember, too, that innuendo serves a particular discourse function because it is indirect. The examples use irony to veil criticism of a coworker, punning to build rapport, and allusion to discuss a taboo topic. The innuendo cannot simply be ignored for a single-frame TL message without some loss of equivalence. The result of course is the potential for misunderstanding and loss of face.

INTERACTIVE ISSUES
While this project was conducted under very controlled circumstances, it did model interactive communication through the characters' dialogue. The information from this theatrical study together with research gathered in the literature review can be applied to everyday interactive interpreting situations.

The interpreter is a participant in the interaction, and as such, he makes decisions that contribute to and affect the communication (Metzger, 1999; Roy, 2000). Roy extensively investigates the impact an interpreter has on turn-taking, that is, the influence on the natural flow relative to turn overlap, offering a turn, or creating a turn. The interpreter also participates as a turn-taker. In so doing, the interpreter manages the communication. "Interpreters are an integral part of the exchange process. Speakers cannot know possible transition moments in other languages, nor can they know what pauses are or how turns end" (Roy, p. 99). This relates to Gumperz's assertion that contextualization cues are culturally bound as well as Hymes' contention that communicative competence is necessary to understand the message. Roy continues, "Thus, two turn-taking systems are operating independently of each other while yet another system, a discourse exchange system, is controlled by an interpreter" (p. 99).

Consider now the effect of an utterance that potentially undermines the exchange system. When an individual produces an utterance containing innuendo, the first potential pitfall for the interpreter is relevance. In an interpreted encounter, the interpreter's production lags behind that of the original speaker (Roy, 2000, p. 76). Moreover, Metzger (1999) presents information in a review of the literature in interpreting that interpreters routinely process the message in "chunks" to produce TL chunks which are different from those in the SL (p. 10). Therefore the utterance may fall short in the area of timeliness that Suls (1983) mentioned as a requisite for humor. This will be particularly obvious when the vehicle for the innuendo is an interruption to the established communication event. That presents a challenge for the interpreter to attempt to reconcile the innuendo with the previous utterance that inspired it. That occurs, of course, only if the interpreter even recognizes the innuendo.

The interpreter may very well simply overlook the speaker's intent. Consider Zajdman's (1995) table of possible outcomes of face-threatening acts (Table 4). Metzger (ibid.) describes the interpreted encounter as an overlapping-dyad (Figure 2). Like Roy, Metzger finds that two communication events are happening simultaneously, with the interpreter involved in each. "As the pivotal point between the two dyads, the interpreter is in a unique position. The interpreter's role within each dyad is essentially to understand what the interlocutor says . . . and to construct information from the other dyadic interaction (p. 181)." In each dyad, the interpreter is the hearer on Zajdman's table. Given the chance for

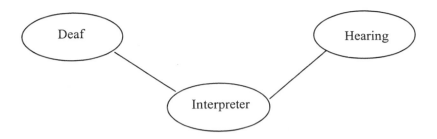

FIGURE 2. *Overlapping-dyad view of interpreting (Metzger, p. 181)*

misunderstanding of the speaker's intent in a one-on-one interaction, consider how that may be exacerbated as the interpreter attends to a second dyad and overall discourse exchange.

This project reveals another important, although less-obvious, interactive issue: the ratified unaddressed participant. Most of the discussion to this point focuses on participants that are ratified and addressed (i.e., participants that match the layman understanding of speaker and listener). Goffman (1981) defines the terms to distinguish those listeners who are an intended part of the communication (ratified) from eavesdroppers and bystanders (unratified). Within the ratified category, a participant might be specifically addressed, leaving the other, still ratified, participants unaddressed. This is evident in settings such as classrooms, staff meetings, and workshops where all the participants are ratified, but a single person might be singled out and addressed for a given period of time. Goffman emphasizes the importance of these distinctions to recognize circumstances such as those wherein not all ratified participants will choose to attend to the message or those in which an unaddressed ratified participant may interject utterances between interchanges sustained by other participants (p. 146).

The Princess Plays with Wood simulated a conversation between Rod P. Longacre and Miss Linda. The script was selected to feature two ratified addressed participants. Twice, however, the illusion of that dyad was broken. Actress B and Interpreter B both addressed the camera. In so doing, they revealed themselves as participants in the communication event rather than merely conduits, and they brought that same ratified status to the audience, which was assumed to be a bystander prior. It is beyond the scope of this project to explore this further, but it is a poignant observation for interpreters. While innuendo may be used in one-on-one interactions like utterances (2) and (3) above, they are just as likely to be used in settings such as the staff meeting in utterance (1). The coworker who interjects the comment about Bob's absence can do so without actually taking the floor. Amidst a dialogue in the "work" frame, the coworker creates the second "play" frame. The other participants react, and one frame or the other will eventually dominate as the participants get back on track or continue joking. Immediately, though, the issue is complicated for the interpreter who now must manage a communication event where some participants accept one frame, and some the other.

Many complications are systemic to the interpreting process. The situation is exacerbated by the issue mentioned above: Innuendo often occurs among people who know each other and converse by drawing upon shared knowledge. "Speaking the same language, in the sense in which that term is understood by linguists, may be enough for short task-oriented instrumental exchanges; but to create conversational involvement and to evaluate intent in longer exchanges, a much greater degree of shared knowledge is necessary" (Gumperz, 1977, p. 207). That may be detrimental to interpreters who are not privy to background information. Innuendo may go unnoticed in the SL or may be produced ineffectively in the TL because of it. For example, if an utterance fraught with innuendo is uttered in a business meeting, the interpreter may prefer to explicate the message if he deems it necessary for accuracy. Being unfamiliar with the attitudes and political climate of that workplace, however, he risks conveying the message in an inappropriate or even offensive way. Notice that utterance (1) and (3) above do not actually say Bob is lazy and Bill is gay, although those intended sentiments are clear to insiders.

Of course interpreters must also be aware of more insidious uses of innuendo in interaction. Hostility may be expressed with veiled insults. As seen in *The Princess Plays with Wood*, innuendo also expresses sexual material powerfully and can be used for harassment. It can target the victim and provide cover for the assailant. In an interpreted encounter, these acts can be all the more blatant because the interpreter can be used as a scapegoat if the addressee challenges the speaker on his utterance. The original speaker can claim the interpreter misconstrued his intent.

Conclusion

To study innuendo, one must investigate numerous components of language that make up—or function as—innuendo. Chief among those are humor and indirectness. For an addressee to understand the speaker's intent, he must have reached a level of communicative competence to recognize the speaker's contextualization cues. Both the cues and the competence to recognize them are culturally bound. Therefore an interpreter working interlingually and cross-culturally will be expected to have the appropriate level of competence in each language. Even so, systemic problems within interpreted encounters will affect the outcome.

Both English and ASL have humor, punning, and indirectness strategies. Anecdotal evidence suggests that ASL also has innuendo, and that it functions similarly—at least in part—in ASL as it does in English. The results of this project suggest, however, that the insinuation is created and signaled differently in each language. Although this investigation is an introductory study, and limited in scope, it did provide worthwhile insights. First, the project highlighted particular strategies that the actresses and interpreters used to convey the English innuendo in ASL. These included:

- using unnamed classifiers,
- fingerspelling the English word containing a double entendre,
- using gesture and facial expressions to suggest doubt or deception,
- choosing TL vocabulary with specific connotations,
- exaggerating sign production to skew or inflect meaning, and
- explicating information that was implied in the SL.

Often the participants used several strategies in tandem to convey the intent of the SL message. Second, the study revealed that each participant created the second frame according to the contextualization cues of their own native language. This is especially important with regard to message equivalence. Key components of innuendo are recognizing and reconciling the contrasting frames. If the TL audience is given a SL contextualization cue, can the rest of the message that follows have equivalent impact? Lastly, the results of this project were combined with information gained from a review of the literature to discuss how this information might influence equivalence and interactive issues in everyday interpreting assignments. While *The Princess Plays with Wood* contains extreme examples of innuendo, interpreters in any setting may have to confront similar kinds of figurative language use.

Suggestions for Future Research

As stated above, future research should investigate the ethnographic role of innuendo in ASL and Deaf culture. This project focused on interpreting

English innuendo into ASL, but do ASL users generate innuendo for their own purposes? If ASL does indeed have innuendo, what function does it serve? Does innuendo in ASL parallel innuendo in English, as euphemisms seemingly do? Answers to these questions lead in turn to the development of more specific strategies for interpreting innuendo between the two languages. Roush (1999) investigated indirect politeness strategies in ASL. A logical follow-up, then is the ethnographic functions of negative indirectness in ASL.

This project was limited to female participants. Obvious issues for future research are whether men and women convey innuendo similarly. With that, does an audience accept similar kinds of utterances from either a man or a woman? For example, if a female interpreter takes on the typically male performance posture to deliver the humor between two male consumers, will the message be received by the TL addressee as intended by the speaker? Remember, the interpreter is the pivot point of two separate dyads. Will the addressee feel comfortable with a traditionally male interaction produced from a female persona? Finally, research to date has focused primarily on addressed participants and their interaction. A study on the impact of ratified unaddressed participants might be enlightening. Unaddressed participants may be a substantial factor for issues such as turn-taking and saving face.

NOTES

1. *Webster's New World Dictionary* 1990.

2. THINK-HEARING describes a deaf individual who is regarded as trying to behave like a hearing person. Analogous to racial situations, it translates roughly to "'wannabe'." GOOD-QUESTION is roughly "'your guess is as good as mine'."

3. The three participants varied slightly, but each signed a two-handed classifier to demonstrate holding something heavy that was perpendicular to the body.

4. In an episode that centered around Jerry's sexual orientation, the characters would follow each reference to being gay with the tag "not that there's anything wrong with that." In (3) above, if Speaker A understood the pop culture reference, he or she would know that B heard the information about Bill's orientation.

REFERENCES

Baker-Shenk, C. & Cokely, D. (1980). *The original green books: American Sign Language—A teacher's resource text on grammar and culture.* Washington, DC: Gallaudet University Press.

Barbe, K. (1993). Isn't it ironic that . . : Explicit irony markers. *Journal of Pragmatics, 20* (6), 579–590.

Boxer, D. & Cortes-Conde, F. (1997). From bonding to biting: Conversational joking and identity display. *Journal of Pragmatics, 27* (3), 275–294.

Colson, H. (2002). Contrast and assimilation in verbal irony. *Journal of Pragmatics, 34* (2), 111–142.

Colston, H. & O'Brien, J. (2000). Contrast and pragmatics in figurative language: Anything understatement can do, irony can do better. *Journal of Pragmatics, 32* (11), 1557–1584.

Dolitsky, M. (1983). Humor and the unsaid. *Journal of Pragmatics, 7* (1), 39–48.

Ervin-Trip, S. (1972). On sociolinguistic rules: Alternation and co-occurrence. In J. Gumperz & D. Hymes (Eds.), *Directions in sociolinguistics* (213–250). New York: Holt.

Fine, G. A. 1983. Sociological approaches to the study of humor. In P. E. McGhee & J. H. Goldstein (Eds.), *Handbook of humor research* (159–181). New York: Springer-Verlag.

Frishberg, N. (1990). *Interpreting: An introduction.* Silver Spring, MD: RID Publications.

Geukens, S. K. J. (1978). Distinction between direct and indirect speech acts: Towards a surface approach. *Journal of Pragmatics, 2* (3), 261–276.

Goffman, E. (1974). *Frame analysis.* New York: Harper Row.

Goffman, E. 1981. *Forms of talk.* Philadelphia: University of Pennsylvania Press.

Grice, H. P. (1975). Logic and conversation. In P. Cole & J. L. Morgan (Eds.), *Syntax and semantics: Speech acts* (41–58). New York: Academic Press.

Gumperz, J. J. (1977). Sociocultural knowledge in conversational inference. In M. Saville-Troike (Ed.), *Linguistics and anthropology* (191–211). Washington, DC: Georgetown University Press.

Hay, J. (2000). Functions of humor in the conversation of men and women. *Journal of Pragmatics, 32*(6), 709–742.

Hymes, D. (1974). *Foundations in sociolinguistics: An ethnographic approach.* Philadelphia: University of Pennsylvania Press.

Hymes, D. 1996. *Ethnography, linguistics, narrative inequality: Toward an understanding of voice.* Bristol, PA: Taylor & Francis.

Klima, E. S. & Bellugi, U. (1980). Wit and poetry in American Sign Language. In W. C. Stokoe (Ed.), *Sign and culture* (105–134). Silver Spring, MD: Linstok Press.

Labov, W. (1972). *Sociolinguistic patterns*. Philadelphia: University of Pennsylvania.

Lane, H., Hoffmeister, R., & Bahan, B. (1996). *A journey into the Deaf-world*. San Diego, CA: DawnSignPress.

Larson, M. (1998). *Meaning-based translation: A guide to cross-cultural equivalence*. Lanham, MD: University Press of America.

Leggit, J. S. & Gibbs, R. W., Jr. (2000). Emotional reactions to verbal irony. *Discourse Processes 29*, 1–24.

Metzger, M. (1999). *Sign language interpreting: Deconstructing the myth of neutrality*.Washington, DC: Gallaudet University Press.

Norrick, N. R. (1994). Involvement and joking in conversation. *Journal of Pragmatics 22* (3/4), 409–430.

Obeng, S. G. (1997). Language and politics: Indirectness in political discourse. *Discourse and Society 8* (1), 49–83.

Padden C. & Humphries, T. (1988). *Deaf in America: Voices from a culture*. Cambridge, MA: Harvard University Press.

Pepicello, W. J. & Weisberg R. W. (1983). Linguistics and humor. In P. E. McGhee & J. H. Goldstein (Eds.), *Handbook of humor research* (59–83). New York: Springer-Verlag.

Raskin, V. (1979). Literal meaning in speech acts. *Journal of Pragmatics 3* (5), 489–495.

Raskin, V. (1985). *Semantic mechanisms of humor*. Dordrecht, Holland: D. Reidel Publishing.

Rosen-Knill, D. F. & Henry, R. (1997). The pragmatics of verbal parody. *Journal of Pragmatics 27* (6), 719–752.

Roush, D. R. (1999). Indirectness strategies in American Sign Language: Requests and refusals. Unpublished research from the Department of American Sign Language, Linguists, and Interpretation of Gallaudet University.

Roy, C. B. (2000). *Interpreting as a discourse process*. New York: Oxford University Press.

Saville-Troike, M. (1998). *The ethnography of communication*. Malden, MA: Blackwell Publishers.

Searle, J. R. (1975). Indirect speech acts. In P. Cole & J. L. Morgan (Eds.), *Syntax and semantics: Speech acts* (59–82). New York: Academic Press.

Shadowbox Cabaret. (1999). *The princess plays with wood*. Columbus, OH: Shadow Holding.

Stokoe, W. (1960). *Sign language structure: An outline of visual communication systems of the American Deaf*. Studies in Linguistics: Occasional Paper No. 8. Buffalo, NY: University of Buffalo.

Suls, J. (1983). Cognitive processes in humor appreciation. In P. E. McGhee & J. H. Goldstein (Eds.), *Handbook of humor research* (39–57). New York: Springer-Verlag.

Tannen, D. (1986). *That's not what I meant! How conversation style makes or breaks relationships*. New York: Ballantine.

Tannen, D. (1990). *You just don't understand: Men and women in conversation*. New York: Ballantine.

Valli, C. & Lucas, C. (1992). *Linguistics of American Sign Language: An introduction*. Washington, DC: Gallaudet University Press.

Zajdman, A. (1995). Humorous face-threatening acts: Humor as strategy. *Journal of Pragmatics, 23*(3), 325–339.

APPENDIX A

The Princess Plays with Wood (abridged)

Setting: A one-on-one interview for Back and Forth, a news program. The host is playing devil's advocate to best-selling children's book writer Miss Linda.

Rod: Hello. I am Rod P. Longacre and this is Back and Forth. Tonight we are joined by the authoress of best-selling children's books, Miss Linda.

ML: Hi.

R: Welcome.

ML: Thank you.

R: Now, some people feel that your books are a bad influence on our children. They claim your books are full of sexual innuendo and blatant erotic content that can easily damage children's innocent minds.

ML: I'm sorry Rod, I guess I'm a little stunned by all this. I have no idea what these people are talking about.

R: OK. I'd like to read a passage from your new book, *The Princess Plays with Wood*. "So one fine day the Princess told her Prince, 'I'm going shopping,' but really she was going to meet Big Bob the carpenter who had a really big tool and knew how to use it."

ML: [innocently] What's wrong with that?

R: [appalled] You are practically saying that it is OK for a woman to have an affair if the other guy has . . . shall we say . . . a bigger jimmy!"

ML: [calmly] Now if you read the next line, you'll see that it says, "The tool was an enormous golden hammer given to Big Bob by a wise old sage. It sparkled like the sun itself, and all people were awestruck upon seeing it."

R: [appeased] Well, I must admit it all sounds pretty innocent *to me*. But what about this, [reading from the book] "On a good day, a day when the sun was bright and the song birds sang, the Princess was quite handy in her own right. She could screw like no one else in the kingdom." [lowering the book] That's right, [appalled again] "she could *screw* like no one else in the kingdom!"

ML: [consoling] Now Rod, it is important to keep these things in perspective. You see, a few passages earlier it says, "The Princess and Big Bob were excitedly building a pair of handsome bookshelves to give the Prince for his birthday. As the Princess watched Big Bob do it, she decided she could help. She took Big Bob's tool in her hands . . ."

R: [interrupting] You see! Right there! *I* don't see a problem with building bookshelves, but others have claimed that children take in these images and subconsciously formulate thoughts . . .

ML: [interrupting] Hold on there! [calming down] I think they are reading into the book what they wish to see in it.

R: [appeased] Well, I am sorry to have to bring up the negative views.

ML: I understand. It's alright. There are a lot of jealous, troubled people in the world.

R: That is so true, Miss Linda. That is why I enjoy your books so much; because they have such happy little endings. Would you mind reading the end of *The Princess Plays with Wood* for us?

ML: [flattered] Oh, I'd love to, Rod. [reading] "And in the wonderful kingdom of goodness and light, the fairies danced and the wood nymphs sang. The Prince admired his beautiful bookshelves and the Princess fucked Big Bob."
        The End

Participant Questionnaire

Deaf _____ Hearing _____

Native Language: ASL _____ English _____

Years of Experience:

      Acting _____

      Interpreting _____ Certification Level _____ Year obtained _____

Briefly describe your acting and/or interpreting training: _____

_____

_____

Briefly describe your acting and/or interpreting experience: _____

_____

_____

	Very			Not at All
Did you find this material humorous in English?	3	2	1	0
Did you find this material humorous in ASL?	3	2	1	0
How difficult was this interpretation/performance?	3	2	1	0
Are you satisfied with the results of your efforts?	3	2	1	0

Ethnographic Research on the Use

of Visually Based Regulators

for Teachers and Interpreters

Susan M. Mather

Recent studies (Winston, 2001; Roy, 2000; Ramsey 1997) reported difficulties experienced by students in participating in interpreted activities, despite the fact that the provision of interpreting services is intended to make primarily aurally oriented learning environments accessible and equal for deaf students. Preliminary observations have shown that how interpreters establish gaze settings and where the interpreters are to be positioned directly affect deaf students' abilities to participate in the classroom activity or answer a question posed by the teacher.

First, this paper will address cultural differences between aurally- and visually-oriented-based environments regarding attention-getting, -focusing, and -maintaining, as well as turn-taking systems. The differences in three communicative events will be discussed. Second, the study will examine and compare seating arrangements in the two types of environments and their effects on students' lines of sight. Finally, the paper will emphasize the importance of the interpreter's reliance on the speaker's behavior to achieve the cross-cultural consistency of the interpreter's and the teacher's roles. This information can be invaluable in the design of training and orientation for teachers and educational interpreters.

LITERATURE REVIEW

Turn-Taking Regulators in Signed Discourse

The function and usage of eye gaze by teachers in deaf classrooms have received some attention in recent sign language studies (e.g., Mather 1987;

1996; 2000). These studies show that one of the important linguistic functions of the use of eye gaze serves to regulate signed discourse. These studies, as detailed below, identify what eye gaze behaviors must be learned in order to get, focus, and maintain students' attention efficiently and effectively.

Baker (1977) found that signers generally make eye contact only at turn relevance points, when the signer with the floor checks for feedback, backchanneling and essentially offering an opportunity to change speaker/signer turns. For instance, Baker observed that a deaf person who uses a signed language for communication would not start a conversation unless the addressee is looking at the signer. Baker distinguished between two different types of eye gaze (i.e., negative eye gaze and positive eye gaze). She explained that if one wishes to continue to talk and does not want to give the other person the floor to take up the turn, then the person will avert their gaze away from the addressee, or vice versa. That is what Baker called negative eye gaze. Positive eye gaze occurs if both parties look at each other. Baker explained, "A person cannot 'say' something and be 'heard' if the other person is not watching . . . therefore this constraint makes eye gaze one of the most powerful regulators in sign language" (1977, p. 13).

As Labov (1984) pointed out, peripheral systems such as the use of prosody, vocal qualifiers, and gestures often serves as the primary means for expressing social and emotional information. Even though the social or emotional information could be verbalized via grammatical mechanisms such as "I am moderately upset with you," Labov found that the grammatical mechanism for conveying social and emotional information has lower changes of success and "listeners would not accept these words at their face value" (p. 43). As Labov stated, peripheral systems are considered linguistic features, as are eye gazes.

Mather (1995) found that deaf students must be taught how to use their eye gaze effectively for various tasks in school settings. Gumperz (1981) indicated that students who were successful in school were the ones who knew how to use such regulators to secure their place in the classroom.

Mehan (1979) suggests that the turn-taking mechanism for classroom discourse is almost exclusively of the "current speaker selects next speaker type"; that is, the teacher normally selects the student who will be next to take a turn, but as soon as the student finishes a turn, the floor automatically returns to the teacher.

Weiner and Devoe (1974) expanded the roles of regulators. They identified four functional regulator types: initiation, continuation, shift, and termination. Initiation regulators are used by the speaker to start an exchange, and by the addressee to evoke a response from the speaker. Continuation regulators include those used by the speaker to indicate that his or her turn will continue despite a short pause, and by the addressee to indicate that he or she is paying attention, so the speaker may continue. The speaker who wishes to relinquish a turn or the addressee who wishes to take a turn both use shift regulators. Termination regulators signal that either the speaker or addressee wishes to end an exchange.

Mather (1996) found that Weiner and Devoe's four types of proposed functional regulators COULD NOT without accommodations be applied effectively to classrooms of deaf students due to their lack of access to auditory information. To get the intended addressee's attention in a deaf classroom, the signer must take appropriate steps whenever necessary. Mather calls these steps pre-initiation regulators. The first step involves finding where the addressee's eye gaze is directed. Regardless of whether the addressee is paying attention, the signer must perform an assessment by asking three basic questions: (1) Is the addressee looking at the signer directly? (2) Is the addressee reading or chatting with someone else yet still within the signer's line of peripheral vision? Or (3) Is the addressee completely out of the signer's line of vision? This is known as eye assessment. Answers to those three questions help to set up the kind of summons technique the signer must use to elicit the addressee's attention.

Mather identified at least three different strategies that the signer can use to summon the intended addressee's attention: visual, eye-level, and tactile. A signer implementing the first strategy will use a visual summons, such as waving or using sharp hand/body motions, to get the addressee's attention. The second strategy involves the use of eye-level attention-getting devices, such as moving into the intended addressee's field of vision slowly and/or using an eye-gaze-level waving summons, depending on what the addressee is doing (facing downward, reading, or gazing upward). The purpose of this gentle eye-level waving is to make sure the addressee is not startled by the signer; thus the signer has to be careful as he or she moves closer to the addressee's field of vision. The third strategy involves tapping the intended addressee's shoulder. This is known as a tactile summons. After summoning and securing the addressee's eye contact, the signer will pause, or wait for the addressee's acknowledgement, before beginning to sign.

Mather (1987) examined the use of eye gaze in self-contained class-rooms for deaf and hard of hearing students and found that the uses of negative eye gaze and positive eye gaze are not the per se types; however, there are certain levels and functions for both eye gaze types. For example, she found that teachers who sign have to employ two different types of positive eye gaze, that is, individual gaze [I-Gaze] and group-indicating gaze [G-Gaze].

If the teacher wishes to speak to a particular student, she would first establish eye contact with the addressee. The other students in the class would know that the teacher is talking to that student. After talking to the student, the teacher would give another type of positive eye gaze, G-Gaze, to the group, signaling that she is now ready to talk to the students as a group. In doing this, she would avert her eye gaze away from the particular student and then evenly direct her eye gaze at all the students, moving her gaze constantly across or around the group without pausing. Correct G-Gaze is performed in a smooth, arc-like motion, with the head turning smoothly from one side of the group to the other.

The G-Gaze can be used to address two people as well as a group. However, the inappropriate use of a certain type of eye gaze may confuse people. In Mather's study, a teacher who was not aware of eye gaze culture signed to her students that they did not know the story, but directed her I-Gaze at one particular student for a brief moment. This student protested strongly and told the teacher that she did know the story well. The teacher replied, "I did not say 'YOU,' and I do know that you know the story. I said THEY do not know the story." Even though the teacher signed the third person pronoun THEY, her individual eye gaze remained directly at the student, not the group. That student felt singled out by the inappropriate I-Gaze and became defensive over the mistaken accusation.

Mather and Thibeault (2000) identified a third type of positive eye gaze as Audience-Gaze (A-Gaze). While both A-Gaze and G-Gaze both denote gazing at a group, A-Gaze applies to a larger group with more than 10 people. Instead of using a smooth, arch-like gaze from right to left, or vice versa (G-Gaze), the speaker using A-Gaze will gaze at the center of the audience so that the audience is being addressed as a unit.

In the audience setting, the signer who wishes to address a particular group or individual would use G-Gaze and I-Gaze, respectively. For instance, the signer using a G-Gaze would thrust his or her head forward or lower and gaze in a smooth, arch-like fashion over the particular group. The signer who wishes to address a particular person in an audience would make direct eye contact with the person to send a signal to the audience and the addressee that the signer is talking specifically to that person. The major difference between A-Gaze and G-Gaze is the former requires less frequency and time of the smooth, arch-like gazes from right to left, or vice versa.

Interpreted Discourse

Recent research on educational interpreting shows that deaf students experienced difficulties in participating in interpreted class activities. For instance, La Bue (1998) reported that deaf students, despite repeated direct calls by the teacher to participate, often saw their role reduced to that of hear-bystanders in their own classrooms.

Roy (2000) and Wadensjö (1988) reported that mainstreaming difficulties are partly due to the faulty assumptions by some teachers that interpreters are the solution to adapting the classroom for a deaf child, and that no further accommodations are necessary. Winston (2001) showed that students who are deaf require visual access to classroom routines, but interpreting by itself does not provide complete visual access. She also reported that certain classroom routines that occur every time lessons and information are exchanged could not be interpreted.

La Bue (1998) examined interpreted discourses in a large middle through high school public school program. In this study, La Bue found that the discourse markers (footing markers) used by teachers to invite students to participate were not conveyed to the deaf students; and as a result, they did not get the invitation to participate.

Literature reviews reveal guidelines and recommendations for the physical location of interpreters in classrooms, but no practical evidence supported one position over another (Kluwin & Stewart, 2001). In fact, as Fleetwood (2000) reports, no clearly defined educational outcome drives any standard of practice where educational signed language interpreting is concerned.

Visual Fields and Classroom Design

Burg's 1968 study demonstrated that the visual field (the area the eye can perceive) is roughly 60 degrees above and below the center and slightly over 90 degrees to the outside (and 60 degrees from the inside for each eye, where it is partially blocked by the nose). The normal lateral visual field (from side to side) is nearly 180 degrees.

Literature on classroom design shows that well-designed classrooms are a critical factor in creating the appropriate environment for effective classroom instruction; one of three fundamental requirements is that the classroom design allows students to see anything presented visually. The other two requirements for a well-designed classroom are that it allows students to hear without noise or distortion and be physically comfortable (Allen et al., 1996).

Classrooms as Culture Settings

Classrooms are complex cultural settings. It is critically important for the teacher and interpreter to understand them as such because learning is an intellectual process, which is socially mediated. This means that learning relies greatly on communication. Since education is dependent on communication between teacher and student, and among students, the teacher and interpreter have important responsibilities to understand and help shape the social contexts for classroom communication.

Culture is defined as knowledge of shared rules (Goodenough, 1965). That knowledge determines communication and sets up social practices in classrooms. In applying the concept of culture to classrooms, Sarason (1971) noted that tacitly held cultural norms and practices make everyday life sensible and meaningful. In this statement, Sarason emphasized the point that deeply in thought, action and social structure within the classroom is the cultural knowledge that rules how to communicate in the classroom.

Gumperz (1981, p. 7) argued that "the importance of the students knowing the behavioral strategies required gaining the teacher's attention or to obtain entry into a place of study and secure cooperation of the peer group." This line of research suggests that to ensure the use of the interpreting process as an effective tool, the teacher and interpreter need to be familiar with the cultural norms and practices for regulating classroom both in aurally and visually oriented modes.

Based on my observations as well as interviews with educators, I have determined that while different cultures exist along the continuum of placements for deaf students, this paper focuses only on two cultures—aurally oriented classrooms and visually oriented classrooms. Aurally oriented

TABLE 1. *Cultural Differences Between Aurally and Visually Oriented Classroom Arrangements*

Typical Classroom Arrangements	Aurally Oriented Classrooms	Visually Oriented Classrooms
Numbers of students	Between 25 and 30	Limited to 10
Shape of classrooms	Rectangle	Square
Seating arrangements	Rows (facing same direction)	U-shape

settings are found mostly in public schools, high schools, and colleges; visually oriented classrooms are found in deaf programs or self-contained classrooms in public schools. It is tempting, but inappropriate, to classify them as *hearing* and *deaf* classrooms, respectively, for several reasons. First, not all teachers in hearing or deaf classrooms use the same rules for turn-taking, getting students' attention, or using visual aids. For instance, teachers in public schools impart both visual and auditory information simultaneously, while hearing students process both at the same time (e.g., demonstrating an object while describing it). Second, not all deaf classrooms are visually oriented per se; in fact, many deaf classrooms use a mixture of visually and aurally oriented approaches.

For the purpose of this paper, I intend to use aurally and visually oriented approaches as follows. The term *aurally oriented classrooms* refers to classrooms where the primary mode of communication is speaking and listening clearly to each other, and good eye contact exists between the teacher and the individual students. (Good eye contact between the students may not be provided in every classroom, depending on the nature of the class.) *Visually oriented classroom* also refers to a setting where the primary mode of communication is sign language and speechreading, and this mode of communication requires good eye contact not only between the teacher and the students but also among the students.

As explained below, the aurally oriented and visually oriented classrooms have their own different rules, procedures, and practices for class participation. Table 1 (on this page) describes the differences in classroom arrangements that I have observed between aurally based and visually based school settings.

Observations show that auditory oriented classrooms are traditionally rectangular in shape, whereas visually oriented classrooms are typically square. The seating arrangements for aurally oriented classrooms are usually composed of several rows facing the front of the classroom, seating as many as 30 students. However, visually oriented classrooms are limited to a capacity of 10, and the seating is arranged in a semicircle so that visual contact can be made with each person in the room.

In an auditory oriented setting, the reasons for setting the desks in rows are two-fold: 1) to provide access to the written information on the blackboard, and 2) to utilize the space in the classroom by arranging it to hold its maximum capacity. This seating arrangement holds less significance than in visually oriented settings, because in an auditory oriented setting, the students rely only on visual stimulus, but not for primary linguistic communication. If the teacher is lecturing while writing information on the blackboard, the students can access visual and auditory instruction simultaneously. Additionally, teachers in this type of classroom are free to walk alongside the students to monitor their work and provide individual feedback. Even though the feedback may only be given to one student at a time, other classmates can still benefit from this instruction since they have access to the auditory information by hearing the conversations between the student and the teacher. Thus, the students may be able to correct their mistakes or add information to their work on the basis of the feedback given to others.

In visually oriented classrooms, the desks are arranged in a U-shape. Because the students rely on visual access, the U-shape allows each person in the classroom to make eye contact with each other as well as read the blackboard. If the seating arrangements were set up in traditional rows, students would not be able to shift their eye gaze quickly to another student during discussion periods and hence would miss out on what was being said.

As discussed earlier, the teacher in the U-shaped seating arrangement can provide one-on-one feedback to students.

In the aurally oriented classroom with rows of seats, the teacher can instruct while standing anywhere in the room, including over the shoulder of a student. In visually oriented classrooms, regardless of the placement of the seats, the teacher must position his- or herself in front of the students so that eye contact is possible.

Thus, the challenge to surmount when using an interpreter in the classroom is, as captured by Hymes (1972),

How to combine two sets of values, two speech communities, so as not to repress personal and community worth, yet give access to means made necessary by forces outside the local community's control (p. liv).

METHODOLOGY

Many studies show that, to serve students' interests, teachers should consider the social dynamics in both the classroom and the communities of which the students are part. In order to gain as broad a picture as possible of the students being served, many researchers have used ethnographic methods. Studies have shown that these methods, which are part of qualitative research, can be useful for examining learning processes and the transmission of culture in the school and community.

Ethnography is a primary approach to data collection and analysis in sociolinguistics; its purpose is to seek to understand and represent the points of view of the members of a particular culture. Dell Hymes (1962) founded the ethnography of speaking, and his primary goal was to survey the full range of speech activities in the communities he would study. This field was extended to comprise communication in general, known as the ethnography of communication (Gumperz & Hymes, 1964; 1972; Bauman & Sherzer, 1974).

The data collected in the field of ethnography are rich in their descriptions of people, places, cultures, languages, and events. In ethnographic studies, researchers conduct extensive fieldwork by listening carefully to what people say, directly observing their cultural behaviors, and studying the products of their behaviors. Doing this, researchers hope to make detailed observations of behavior with careful control of possible sources of bias and distortion.

Various education researchers have used this method in education. Cazden, Hymes, and John (1972) used ethnographic methods to research language use and its social functions in the classroom. Erickson and Mohatt (1982) employed ethnographic tools such as direct observation, videotaping, and interviews to observe the organization of social relationships in two classrooms of culturally similar children whose teachers had different cultural backgrounds from theirs.

Ethnographic methods have been used to examine the education of deaf students as well (Mather, 1987; 1996). In these studies, Mather used direct observation, videotaping, and interviews to study the attention-getting and attention-maintaining strategies used by culturally different teachers who used sign language in story reading.

Ethnographic research is described as a multi-instrumental approach. A cornerstone of ethnographic methodology is participant observation, in which the observer becomes part of the community being studied so as to understand what is happening and what the subjects see. A number of ethnographic studies required researchers to spend years working as participant observers in the communities they studied. Heath (1983), for instance, spent several years examining the literacy tasks that people in two distinct communities used to understand their use of oral and written language and how that use might influence classroom practices. Michael Armstrong (1980) spent an entire school year observing and teaching children in a British primary school class to study intellectual growth and its enabling conditions.

In addition to participant observation, data gathering techniques include note-taking, videotaping, and interviewing informants. Ethnographic studies do not revolve around testing pre-established hypotheses, but rather around trying to describe in detail all the aspects of communication in a given setting(s) at issue. In keeping with the nature of qualitative research design, this study is, in the words of Creswell (2003, p. 181), "emergent, rather than tightly prefigured."

For this study, the data include participant observations from undergraduate and graduate studies at the Rochester Institute of Technology, Gallaudet University, and Georgetown University. At Gallaudet University, presentations given in the auditorium were interpreted. At Georgetown, interpreted settings included group discussions and classroom lectures. At the National Technical Institute for the Deaf (NTID), the settings reviewed included lecture rooms and large and small classrooms. At times, two interpreters were provided, especially in classes that lasted at least one hour.

In three classes, with the teachers' permission, I discussed with the interpreters their appropriate placements in the classrooms, depending on the physical layout of the classroom and the type of classroom activity. We also discussed their postures and gaze settings, as well as any possible accommodations that could be made, based on the teacher's teaching strategies.

Most of the students and interpreters were interviewed at least once over the course of the classes. The resulting data set includes field notes, interview write-ups, and a set of videotapes, which captures various small- and large-group classes. I continue to develop and expand notes, and other documents relative to my analysis.

The data also include informal interviews with students, interpreters, and teachers in the past decade. These people were selected for interviews through solicitation and by word of mouth. Since the purpose is to explore, gain understanding, and generate theory about the use and location of interpreters in classrooms, we selected cases that would be good examples. These cases were telling because they were showed how interpreting services could be effective, because of the teachers', interpreters', and students' levels of experience as well as their attitudes toward and knowledge of education interpreters, and their willingness to share their ideas and experiences. Their experiences vary from elementary to postsecondary programs. The case studies include classroom observations. The data collected included video recordings of the teachers along with the interpreters.

Data collection included interviews with teachers in visually oriented self-contained classes regarding effective teaching strategies in major subject areas. In keeping with qualitative research design, this study was interpretive. According to Creswell (2003, p. 182), when conducting a qualitative study such as this, "the researcher filters the data through a personal lens that is situated in a specific sociopolitical and historical moment. One cannot escape the personal interpretation brought to qualitative data analysis." I have sought to assemble specific participant answers to various questions about communication to differentiate the significant "differences between answers which reflect cultural ideals or norms and the real or what actually occurs" (Saville-Troike, 1994, p. 118).

ANALYSIS

My central concern in studying interpreted classrooms has been the interpreters' interpretation of the teachers' use of class routines, gaze settings, and their placements within three types of classroom activities: general-purpose, group discussions, and lectures.

Attention-Getting Strategies in Interpreted Classes

I have studied the uses of I-Gaze, G-Gaze, and A-Gaze by interpreters in various educational activities.

During the 1980s, personal observations of placements for interpreters and students who relied on interpreting services showed that it was once standard practice for interpreters to sit on the left or right corner of the speaker's stage, and for the students to sit on the corresponding side of the room that provided the best distance and angle for seeing the interpreter. The same data also show that these interpreter and student placements were set without taking into consideration whether the students had a good angle for seeing the speaker or other students in the room.

The data also indicate that how interpreters view their role determines their eye gaze settings. Specifically, the data reveal that the eye gaze settings of interpreters in these placements were consistently directed at the student(s). This reality ignores data suggesting that eye gaze functions linguistically (Baker, 1977) and, therefore, should be employed without regard for who hires the interpreter.

The data shows that in those situations involving one deaf participant, the interpreter used I-Gaze, and in other situations with two or more students, the interpreter used G-Gaze. Interviews with the participants reveal that they disliked the interpreter's gaze and placement within the room. Some students commented that they felt like they were being watched or singled out. Some of the interpreters commented that they were being forced to watch the students and sign at the same time.

In essence, both the participants and the interpreters agreed that it seemed unnatural for them to look at each other all the time. For instance, one deaf student asked, "Why does the interpreter have to STARE-AT-US?" When the student asked the interpreters the question, the interpreters replied that they worked for the deaf participants only. The deaf students held a different opinion on the role of the interpreters in the classroom. One student said, "They [interpreters] are here to interpret for speakers only." I asked the students if the interpreters were not here to interpret for the students. One student replied that the interpreters were hired because the speaker could not sign, and therefore, the interpreters were hired to interpret for the speaker, not the deaf students.

Interviews with the interpreters reveal their understanding that they were hired because the deaf students asked for them. The interpreters said that they had to gaze at the students to ensure student comprehension.

TABLE 2. *Differences in Attention-Getting Strategies for Calling One or More Students*

Teacher's calls	Aurally oriented classrooms	Visually oriented classrooms
Before the class starts (initiation regulators)	Announcing audibly at beginning the class simultaneously	Getting group gaze before beginning the class
To get a student's attention	By name	Individual gaze and visual/tactile summons
To get a group's attention	Vocal regulators (cues such as "um")	Group-indicating gaze and visual/tactile summons

The interpreters also commented that they felt responsible to make sure that the students were paying attention to what "I" [the speaker] said.

These discussions reveal a conflict on cultural views on the roles of interpreters. These discussions pose several issues for further study. When the teacher attempts to get the hearing students' attention (through more passive or more active means), is it the interpreter's responsibility to use culturally appropriate visual methods of equal force (more passive or more active) for getting deaf students' attention? Also, as with the hearing students, is it the teacher's responsibility to determine whether students (hearing and deaf) are actually paying attention after being summoned to do so? Should teachers in aurally oriented classrooms be taught to recognize what it means for a deaf student to pay attention (e.g., they must be looking at the source of information and/or at the interpreter)? Should the role of the interpreter be consistent with the speaker's role— that is, should the interpreter use similar gazes that the speaker uses? For instance, should the interpreter use A-Gaze when the speaker addresses the audience, G-Gaze when the speaker addresses a group within a group, and I-Gaze at the intended individual to whom the speaker speaks?

Attention-Getting Regulators in Interpreted Settings

Observations showed cultural differences between attention-getting norms in the aurally oriented environment and those in the visually oriented

TABLE 3. *Cultural Differences in Asking and Answering from Students*

Teachers' question-asking period (shift initiation regulators)	Aurally oriented classrooms	Visually oriented classrooms
Pace of questioning and answering	Overlap at teacher's discretion	Overlap discouraged
Numbers of students' answers	As many as four students' answers at various times	One at a time
Recognizing who is answering	Voice recognition	Visual recognition

environment. For instance, in the aurally oriented classroom, people greeted one another by calling their names. In the visually oriented environment, instead of greeting with a name-calling, a signer made direct eye contact with the addressee. Once eye contact was established, the greeter signed HELLO.

Table 2 shows the difference between the ways teachers called on their students in aurally and visually oriented classrooms before instruction resumed.

As an example, the data show that in one aurally oriented classroom, the teacher employed initiation regulators by using one of the vocal paralinguistic initiation regulators, "umm," or calling a student's name and saying, "Let us start the lesson today." When the other students heard the teacher calling out, they immediately knew the class has begun. Whether the students were busy talking or reading, they had access to the auditory information that class has started.

The aurally based attention-getting strategies do not apply to visually based classrooms. The data revealed that in a number of cases, the teachers used various means of visual and tactile regulators to get each student's attention. In some cases, teachers switched the lights on and off a few times to get everyone's attention. The teachers would wait until all the students signaled that they were paying attention before they initiated the classes. In these cases, the teachers used the I-gaze strategy instead of the name-calling method used in the aurally oriented classroom.

Personal communications with former students who are deaf show that one of the most common student complaints is that speakers and teachers do not always check to see if the interpreter and deaf participants are ready to listen (personal communications with Jon Hendricks, October 20, 2002). While vocal attention-getting methods are not always effective with hearing students, such methods are, nevertheless, accessible to them.

These findings indicate that in each mode, aural or visual, there is a way for getting attention; and an interpreter who uses a different mode must be cognizant of this in both modes, and interpret it (as well as interpreting actual utterances). Metzger (1999) suggests that there are elements of discourse that must be interpreted, which are not actual utterances. For example, she points out that interpreters should always indicate the source of each utterance, since mono-modal language users know who is talking/signing. Students, deaf or hearing, should have that information as well.

The findings suggest that both teacher and interpreter should resolve the issue of getting deaf students' attention in the mainstreaming setting. How should an interpreter be ready and then subsequently use visual attention-getting strategies? Or should the teacher alert the deaf students directly by waving at them to let them know that the class is about to start before they make a verbal announcement? Or, should the teacher ask the interpreter to see if both the student and interpreter were ready for the class?

In short, the data suggests that while it is the teacher's primary responsibility to get the class's attention, it is also the interpreter's responsibility to make visible that which is otherwise acoustic. This raises two issues: How an interpreter employs appropriate visual attention-getting techniques, and how a teacher can effectively assess the result of those techniques (whether the deaf student pays attention or not). Fleetwood and Metzger (forthcoming) suggest that these responsibilities/standards are long overdue for educational interpreters, and a requirement for interpreter education, certification, and practice. Determining the most effective method will require further study.

Asking and Eliciting Answers from Students in Interpreted Classes

Because the protocol for turn-taking during group discussion is ordinarily controlled by the teacher, who selects a student to take a turn, the initiation and shift regulators are used more often than the other two types of regulators, continuation and termination. Therefore, asking a student a question is very common in the classroom. The way hearing students in public schools answer the teacher's question is far different from the way deaf students answer questions in self-contained, visually oriented classrooms. Table 3 is a summary of the cultural differences in asking and answering from students between aurally and visually oriented classrooms.

In an aurally oriented classroom, there can be multiple students volunteering an answer. If everyone answers correctly, the teacher would acknowledge the group. If only one of them gets the right answer, then the teacher would only acknowledge the student whose answer is correct. The students are allowed to continue giving out various answers quickly until the teacher finally acknowledges the right answer. In this environment, the entire class benefits from the information, and they are able to filter the answers and determine which response is accurate. This method is frequently utilized to prepare students for upcoming exams. This style of questioning and answering and turn-taking is fast-paced (Wilson, 1997). The hearing students have an advantage over the deaf students in that as many as four of them can call out answers and be recognized. They do not have to "see" who is answering since overlapping vocal information is simultaneously available. In addition, the teacher of hearing students can hear answers all over the room in spite of having only two ears. This does not work at all for a teacher of deaf students because he or she has to use both eyes to watch each student's comment at a time. This seems to affect the teacher's teaching styles.

In visually oriented classrooms, instead of allowing several students to answer simultaneously due to the constraint of eye gaze, Mather (1987; 1995; 1996) found that teachers would ask various questions—as many as 15 to one student—until she finally answered. Mather hypothesized that it was easier for the group to watch one student give out multiple possible answers and see which answer is correct. The student has to refocus her gaze every time she shifts her gaze from one person to another (as must the students). As soon as the student volunteers to answer, the teacher has to make sure everyone can see the student's signing space before the teacher nods to the student to begin answering. Because of this differing dynamic in deaf classrooms, group discussions are still limited to one speaker at a time in spite of the U-shaped seating arrangement. Students still need some time to refocus their pupils before they can signal that they are ready to listen.

Interviews with deaf students who attended public schools reveal difficulties that they always experienced difficulty following group discussions due to the fast pace, the difficulty of identifying who is speaking, and their dependence on visual cues in spite of how well they can hear or speak (Personal communication with Brown; Hendricks; Smith). Wilson (1997) pointed out that her deaf subjects admitted that the pace in the hearing classroom is faster than in the deaf classroom, and the sensitivity of meeting individual students' needs in the hearing classrooms is almost null as well.

This discussion shows that the use of turn-taking mechanisms is very different for both groups due to the teachers' ability to hear various answers at various times and the students' ability to recognize the voices. Hearing students have been trained to absorb information as quickly as possible. In contrast, teachers of deaf students cannot allow more than one student to answer at a time because he or she has to depend on both eyes in order to watch one student signing, and vice versa with students. Due to the constraint of having to rely on one's eyes, the pace of turn-taking in deaf classrooms is much more restricted and controlled than in hearing classrooms.

Interpreters' Placement within Classrooms

Preliminary observations have shown that it is customary for a deaf student to sit in the middle of the front row with an educational interpreter next to the teacher's position (see Figure 1). This seating arrangement, however, poses difficulties for the deaf student to participate in class discussion. For instance, the seating arrangement does not provide appropriate lines of sight for the deaf student to see other students during the class discussion, requiring either the teacher or the interpreter to notify the deaf student of which student is taking a turn or being addressed by the teacher. Crucial to effective participation is a deaf student's access to the panoramic view of the classroom.

To ensure that deaf students have a panoramic view of their teacher, interpreter, and classmates to the maximum extent possible, the teacher should consider possible classroom accommodations (as shown in Figures 2 and 3).

Figure 2 represents an ideal seating arrangement for deaf students in a mainstreaming setting. This configuration allows the deaf student to have

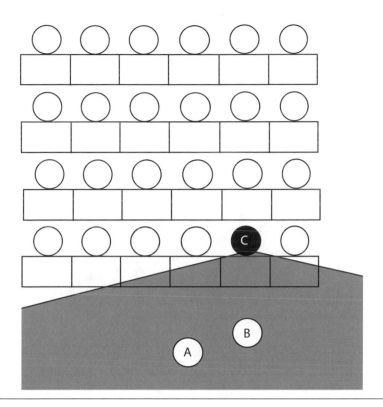

FIGURE 1. *Interpreted 24-Student Classroom with a Deaf Student Sitting in the Second Left Front Chair*

A =   Instructor
B =   Interpreter
C =   Deaf student
Shaded area =   The student's vision field

sight lines to the teacher, the interpreter, and his or her peers without relying on the teacher or interpreter for clues.

If the U- or V-shape seating arrangement is not possible due to fixed chairs, too small a room, or a large number of students, the teacher should consider the second classroom accommodation (as shown in Figure 3). The configuration shown in Figure 3 should also be considered for general-purpose activities with emphasis on lectures. In this arrangement, deaf students should have a swivel chair so that the student can face sidewise.

Figure 4 shows possible class accommodations for group discussions. Preliminary observations demonstrate that during group discussions, the

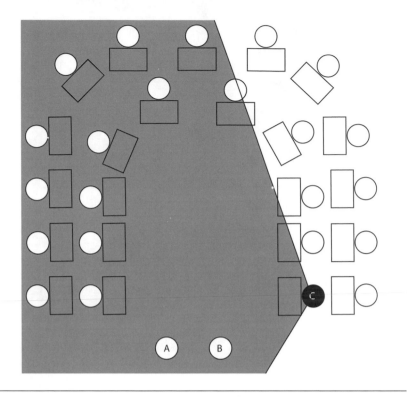

FIGURE 2. *Interpreted 24-Student Classroom with a U- or V-Shape Seating Arrangement*

A = Instructor
B = Interpreter
C = Deaf student
Shaded area = The student's vision field

teacher tended to walk around the room while the deaf student sat in the front of the row with the interpreter sitting in the front of the class. It appears that such an arrangement did not provide the deaf student an opportunity to see who was talking, the group's reaction, etc. As is shown in Figure 4, the deaf student sits in the middle of the last row, provided that the interpreter accompany the teacher all the time or stand next to whoever is talking at the moment.

As was discussed earlier, the objective of the last four classroom accommodations is to provide the deaf student with a panoramic view of the class activities to ensure that they have the benefits of observing and participating in the activities.

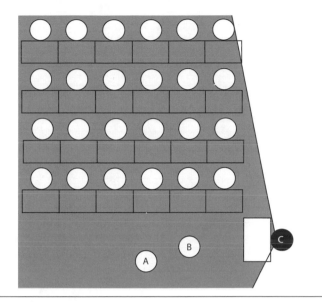

FIGURE 3. *Interpreted 24-Student Classroom Fixed Seating Arrangement–Lecture-Type Activities*

A = Instructor
B = Interpreter
C = Deaf student
Shaded area = The student's vision field

Three Observed Communicative Events

The following are my observations of the three different communicative events—classroom lectures, group discussions, and platform lectures relative to the principles discussed above.

The First Observed Communicative Event: Classroom Lecture

The first communicative event involved a lecture on language variation given by a professor in a very large classroom with more than 50 unfixed seats. During the lecture, the students were expected to sit and listen with no questions or interruptions allowed. The professor established the A-gaze setting for her lecture. However, the interpreter used I-Gaze at the deaf student. After the class, when I asked why she used I-Gaze instead of A-Gaze, the interpreter explained that she had to watch the deaf student to make sure that she was following her interpretation. I asked the

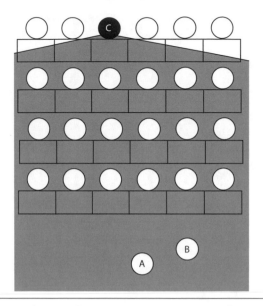

FIGURE 4. *Interpreted 24-Student Group Discussion in a Classroom with Rows of Fixed Seats*

A = Instructor
B = Interpreter
C = Deaf student
Shaded area = The student's vision field

student how she felt being gazed at individually. She expressed discomfort. In the next class, I proposed that the interpreter use the gaze consistent with the professor's gaze—that is, the A-gaze. In the next class, the interpreter employed the A-Gaze, with I-Gaze periodically, to make sure that the student was following her interpretations. Following the second class, the interpreter expressed feelings of ambivalence toward the use of A-Gaze because she was signing to an audience who did not know sign language. On the other hand, the student no longer felt that she was being stared at and now saw herself as part of the group. The student also felt that the interpreter was interpreting accurately what the professor said and reflecting the professor's style of lecture.

The Second Observed Communicative Event: Group Discussion

A group discussion following a professor's lecture on discourse analysis included approximately 30 students. In this class, the interpreter sat in front of the room facing the students and next to the standing professor, which is similar to Figure 1. In this case, the interpreter used A-Gaze, and the deaf student sat in the front row. There were several rows of seats behind the deaf student, similar to Figure 1. The professor established ground rules for discussion: Only one individual would speak at a time, and no overlapping discussion would be allowed. In the beginning of one class, the professor posed a question using the A-Gaze. The interpreter used the same gaze setting. Once the discussion started, the professor used I-Gazes at those individual students who took the turn to speak. The interpreter used the A-Gaze. The deaf student, however, was confused by who was speaking, who was taking the turn, and to whom the next speaker was addressing mostly due to the fact that the professor did not mention the names of each student who spoke. This problem was also compounded by the fact that the changes in turn-taking were so rapid that the interpreter did not have an opportunity to tell the deaf student who was taking the turn.

Another difficulty experienced by the deaf student was that when she engaged in discussion, she was talking to the interpreter—even when she was responding to another student's comment. Due to the vision limits imposed by the interpreter's and the deaf student's placement within the classroom, the deaf student was unable to face the student who made a comment to which the deaf student was responding.

After discussing the issues, the professor, deaf student, and interpreter agreed to accommodate the group discussion by moving the interpreter to the side of the classroom and turning the deaf student's chair to face the entire class. This arrangement is similar to that depicted in Figure 3. The deaf student reported that she was now able to see who was talking, who the next speaker was, and to whom the speaker was addressing while discussing a specific issue. During the group discussion, the interpreter used similar gazes and shifted her body postures consistent with the speakers' and listeners' body postures. For instance, if the individual spoke to the professor, the interpreter used I-Gaze toward the professor from the speaker's standpoint, indicating to the deaf student that the speaker was addressing the teacher. When the professor spoke to the class using the A-Gaze, the interpreter used the A-Gaze toward the class, showing that the professor was addressing the class as a group. When two students took their turns speaking, the interpreter shifted her head and body posture, indicating that turn-taking had occurred.

The class rearrangement also allowed the deaf student to face and speak to a previous speaker directly. Also, when the professor was addressing the deaf student, the interpreter shifted her body posture toward and used I-Gaze at the deaf student, indicating to her that she was being addressed by the professor. The interpreter used similar procedures when one student was asking or talking to the deaf student.

The Third Observed Communicative Event: The Platform Lecture

I observed the following communicative events, platform lectures, which were given in an auditorium. Preliminary observations showed that in these events, interpreters were asked to sit on the floor of the auditorium, not on top of the platform with the speaker.

After discussing the issues of eye gaze settings and placements with members of the deaf community, interpreters agreed to the deaf participants' requests for different arrangements by standing next to the speaker on the platform. The deaf participants also requested a different seating arrangement and instead sat in other parts of the audience. During the lecture, the speaker used A-Gaze when addressing the audience, G-Gaze when talking to a group within the audience, and I-Gaze when speaking to an individual; the interpreters used gaze settings consistent with each speaker. Subsequent interviews showed that the deaf participants did not feel singled out, but instead felt like members of the audience, not at all restricted by the interpreters' placements during the lecture.

The findings of this study reveal the importance of cross-cultural consistency between the speaker's role, behaviors, and eye gaze settings, as well as those of the interpreter.

CONCLUSION

As is shown above, ethnographic methods have proven highly successful for providing insights into various interpreted classroom experiences and the range of classroom accommodations required to ensure effective interpretations. This information can be invaluable in the design of future research into the interpreting process, as well as training and educational programs for educational interpreters.

Inquiry into other routines teachers and interpreters use in classrooms can provide information on their performance and the effects on deaf students' abilities to participate effectively in classroom activities. For instance, a teacher or an interpreter can investigate whether particular accommodations should be made to serve the interests of deaf students regarding using props for demonstration purposes; writing on the blackboard as part of instruction; showing a film, slide show, or videotape with class discussion, using overhead projector/PowerPoint presentations, or using a book. In summary, the use of ethnographic methods allows a clearer understanding of interactions among the teachers, students, and interpreters who promote or inhibit communication.

REFERENCES

Alexieva, B. (1997). A typology of interpreter-mediated events. *Translator, 3* (3), 153–174.

Allen, R. L., Bowen, J. T., Clabaugh, S., DeWitt, B. B., Francis, J., Kerstetter, J. P. & Reick, D. A. (1996). *Classroom design manual* (3d ed.). College Park: University of Maryland, Educational Technology Center.

Armstrong, M. (1980). *Closely observed children.* London: Chameleon Books.

Baker, C. (1977). Regulators and turn-taking in American Sign Language. In L. Friedman (Ed.), *On the other hand,* (pp. 215–236). New York: Academic Press.

Bauman, R., & Sherzer, J. (Eds.). (1974). *Explorations in the ethnography of speaking.* Cambridge, UK: Cambridge University Press.

Burg, A. (1968). *Vision test scores and driving record: Additional findings* (Report No. 68-27). Los Angeles: Department of Engineering, University of California.

Cazden, C., Hymes, D., & John, V. (1972). *Functions of language in the classroom.* New York: Teachers College Press.

Creswell, J. (2003). *Research design: Qualitative, quantitative, and mixed methods approaches* (2d ed.). Thousand Oaks, CA: Sage Publications.

Erickson, F. and Mohatt, G. (1982). The social organization of participant structures in two classrooms of Indian students. In G. D. Spindler (Ed.), *Doing the ethnography of schooling: Educational anthropology inaction* (pp. 132–174). New York: Holt, Rinehart, & Winston.

Fleetwood, E. (2000). Educational policy and signed language interpretation. In M. Metzger (Ed.), *Bilingualism and identity in deaf communities* (pp. 161–183). Washington, DC: Gallaudet University Press.

Fleetwood, E., & Metzger, M. (Forthcoming). Standards of practice in educational interpreting. In E. Winston (Ed.), *Educational interpreting: How it can succeed.* Washington, DC: Gallaudet University Press.

Goodenough, W. (1965). Rethinking "status" and "role": Toward a general model of the cultural organization of social relationships. In M. Spiro (Ed.), *The relevance of models for social anthropology* (pp. 1–22). New York: Praeger.

Gumperz, J. & Hymes, D. (1964). The ethnography of communication. *American Anthropologist 66* (6).

Gumperz, J. & Hymes, D. (1972). *Directions in sociolinguistics: Ethnography of communication* (pp. 35–71). New York: Holt, Rinehart & Winston.

Gumperz, J. (1981). Conversational inference and classroom learning. In J. L. Green and C. Wallat (Eds.), *Ethnography and language in educational settings* (pp. 3–23). Norwood, NJ: Ablex.

Heath, S. B. (1983). *Ways with words.* Cambridge,UK: Cambridge University Press.

Hymes, D. (1962). The ethnology of speaking. In T. Gladwin and W. C. Sturtevant (Eds.), *Anthropology and education.* Washington, DC: Anthropological Society of Washington.

Hymes, D. (1972). Models of the interaction of language and social life. In J. J. Gumperz & D. Hymes (Eds.), *Directions in sociolinguistics: Ethnography of communication* (pp. 35–71). New York: Holt, Rinehart & Winston.

Kluwin, T. and Stewart, D. A. (2001). Interpreting in schools: A look at research. *Odyssey 5* (1), 15–17.

La Bue, M. A. (1998). Interpreted education: A study of deaf students' access to the content and form of literacy instruction in a mainstreamed high school English class. *Dissertation Abstracts International, 59* (04), 1057. (UMI No. 9830061)

Labov, W. (1984). Field methods of the project on linguistic change and variation. J. Baugh & J. Sherzer (Eds.), *Language in use: Readings in sociolinguistics*(pp. 28–53). Englewood Cliffs, NJ: Prentice-Hall.

Mather, S. (1987). Eye gaze and communication in a deaf classroom. *Sign Language Studies, 54,* 11–30.

Mather, S. (1995).Pragmatics of eye gaze in deaf classrooms using American Sign Language. Unpublished manuscript, Gallaudet Research Institute, Culture and Communication Studies Program, Washington, DC.

Mather, S. (1996). Initiation in visually constructed dialogue: Reading books with three- to eight- year-old students who are deaf and hard of hearing. In C. Lucas (Ed.), *Multicultural Aspects of Sociolinguistics in in Deaf Communities* 109–131. Sociolinguistics in Deaf Communities series, vol. 2. Washington, DC: Gallaudet University Press.

Mather, S. & Thibeault, A. (2000). Creating an involvement-focused style in book reading with deaf and hard of hearing students: The visual way. In C. Chamberlain, J. P. Morford, & R. Mayberry (Eds.), *Language acquisition by eye* (pp. 191–219). London: Lawrence Erlbaum Associates.

Mehan, H. (1979). *Learning lessons.* Cambridge, MA: Harvard University Press.

Patrie, C. (1993). A confluence of diverse relationships: Interpreter education and educational interpreting. In C. Nettles (Ed.), *Confluence of diverse relationships: Proceedings of the thirteenth national conventions of the Registry of Interpreters for the Deaf* (pp. 3–18). Silver Spring, MD: RID Publications.

Ramsey, C. (1997). *Deaf children in public school: Placement, context, and consequences.* Washington, DC: Gallaudet University Press.

Rodriquez, Y. (2002). Toddlerese: Conversations between deaf Puerto Rican parents and hearing toddlers. *Dissertation Abstracts International 63* (01), 78. (UMI No. 3037921).

Roy, C. (2000). *Interpreting as a discourse process.* Oxford Studies in Sociolinguistics. New York: Oxford University Press.

Sarason, S. B. (1971). *The culture of the school and the problem of change.* Boston: Allyn & Bacon.

Saville-Troike, M. (1994). *The ethnography of communication: An introduction* (2nd ed.). Cambridge, MA: Blackwell Publishers.

Schein, J. D., Mallory, B. L., & Greaves, S. (1991). *Communication for deaf students in mainstream classrooms.* Alberta, Canada: University of Alberta, Edmonton.

Sofinski, B. Yesbeck, N., Gerhold, S., & Christensen Bach-Hansen, M. (2001). Features of voice-to-sign transliteration by educational interpreters. In D. Watson (Ed.), *Journal of Interpretation: Millennial edition.* Alexandra, VA: RID Publications.

Wadensjö, C. (1998). *Interpreting as interaction.* New York: Addison Wesley Longman.

Weiner, M. & Devoe, S. (1974). *Regulators, channels, and communication disruption.* Research Manuscript, Clark University, Worcester, MA.

Wilson, C. (1997). Deaf secondary students' perspectives on educational in mainstream and residential schools: A qualitative interview study. *Dissertation Abstracts International 57* (10), 4329. (UMI No. 9708209).

Winston, E. (2001). *Visual inaccessibility: The elephant (blocking the view) in interpreted education.* http://clerccenter.gallaudet.edu/Odyssey/Winter-Spring2001/visual-inaccessibility.pdf.

A Study of the Complex Nature of

Interpreting with Deaf Students in

Higher Education

Frank J. Harrington

Study and research related to the U.K. deaf community and their language is a relatively new phenomenon, dating back only to the mid 1970s. The first studies focused on the effects of auditory deprivation on children, their intellect, and their education (Brennan, 1976; Kyle, 1978; 1979; 1980). With the establishment of the Centre for Deaf Studies at Bristol University in 1979, and, at around the same time, a research project based at the Moray House Institute, Edinburgh, the focus moved from audiology and language acquisition to questions about the nature of British Sign Language (BSL) and the community of deaf people who used that language as their first or preferred mode of communication (Brennan, Colville, & Lawson, 1980; Brennan & Hayhurst, 1981; Kyle & Woll, 1983; 1985).

This research, and the resulting publications, coincided with the establishment of the Council for the Advancement of Communication with Deaf People (CACDP) in 1981, whose role was to administer the assessment of nationally recognized BSL qualifications and a register of BSL-English interpreters. One result of this period of development was that many people who previously had no connections with the deaf community, or knowledge of BSL, began attending BSL classes and attaining CACDP qualifications. Over the next few years, a significant number of these new BSL learners progressed through the different stages of BSL attainment offered by the CACDP qualifications, and, although no formal training for interpreters was available, many began providing interpreting services to the deaf and hearing communities and became members of the first register of interpreters. The next natural step was for interpreter training programs to be established, and this began to happen in the late 1980s, firstly at Bristol and Durham Universities, then within the Royal National Institute for Deaf People (RNID), Wolverhampton University, and the University of Central Lancashire. Fifteen years on, BSL-English interpreting is still very much in its infancy, and is only now establishing itself as a recognized profession (Pollitt, 1997). So, it is little wonder that published research into interpreting in the U.K., to date, has been limited.

Since the mid 1990s, a handful of studies, focusing specifically on BSL-English interpreting, have been undertaken. This paper will describe one such study, carried out at the University of Central Lancashire (UCLAN).

METHODOLOGY

This paper describes a study, titled "Towards a Whole Institution Approach to Disability and Deafness," addressing interpretation within the higher educational classroom. The study was carried out at UCLAN between 1997 and 1999 and was based on videotaped data, collected over one academic year, in classrooms where a BSL-English interpreter was working to facilitate communication between hearing lecturers and a group of students, at least one of whom was deaf, to give deaf students access to the content of their education.

Theoretical Framework

The leading paradigm for early research into spoken language interpreting, as noted by Gile (1995), was largely cognitive or experimental in focus, seeking to describe the mental processes involved in the act of interpreting, or to test the number and types of errors committed by interpreters. Some of the first researchers studying signed language interpretation followed a similar developmental progression to that of the wider field, carrying out cognitive studies and studies based on error analysis (Cokely, 1992).

More recently, the focus of spoken language interpreting research has changed, with researchers such as Berk-Seligson (1990) and Wadensjö (1992) offering a somewhat different perspective. As Mason (1999, pp.159–160) points out, these researchers have chosen to move "away from concern with the measurement of 'interpreter error,' 'correctness,' 'equivalence' and so on, and thus away from a narrow source-text/target-text comparison towards a more procedural account . . . the interpreter [is seen] as a gatekeeper, coordinator and negotiator of meanings within a three-way interaction." Studies of signed language interpretation (Roy, 1989; 2000; Metzger, 1995; 1999; Brennan & Brown, 1997; Napier, 2002) have also featured in the development of this procedural approach.

This study reflects the shift towards a procedural approach to the study of interpreted interaction. In the introduction to their book *Researching Language: Issues of Power and Method*, Cameron et al. (1992) suggest that research such as this should be "on, for and with" all stakeholders, including interpreters. The effects of this approach on studies of signed language interpreting in the U.K. is reported elsewhere (Turner & Harrington, 2000), but it is important to say here that the adoption of such an approach enables the researchers to actively involve the stakeholders in the various stages of a project, with the effect that stakeholders can feel empowered by the research and share in the success of its findings. The intention is to treat stakeholders essentially as participants or co-researchers rather than simply as passive "subjects" of research.

In keeping with this approach, it was important that the UCLAN study did not focus on an individual interpreter's possible lack of skill, but upon the interpreted event as a whole. Any other approach might have led the researchers to focus on interpreter errors or miscues (Cokely, 1992), rather than on the event as a whole. The study began with the assumption that the interpreter in any given event was competent, and, as a result, the various communication and interactional difficulties that were observed could be found to have originated not only in the actions of the interpreter, but in the complex inter-relationships between all of the participants and their environment. By analyzing the relationships and dynamics that existed between lecturers, students, interpreters, and their environment, the study hoped to identify the type of difficulties with which individuals are faced, and the interactive negotiations that they might need to employ, in order to work with each other more effectively.

Finally, the study, while assuming that every event would be unique, was not looking to identify individual or isolated occurrences, but rather it was looking for trends—things that happened a number of times in the data. This was a qualitative, exploratory study of interpreted interaction. Later on in this paper, I will illustrate some of the trends found in the data, discussing three examples taken from the transcripts.

Signed language interpreting in higher education has a far lower profile in the U.K. than, for example, legal or theatre interpreting. Also, much of the research carried out before the UCLAN study focused mainly on the funding and provision of interpreting services (Higher Education Funding Council for England [HEFCE], 1996) rather than on the complex nature of the task or the effects of interpretation on classroom interaction. The funding for many of these projects came from the HEFCE. From 1993 onwards, HEFCE funded a series of projects that were designed to address issues of access for disabled students, among them, deaf students.

By the time HEFCE announced the third round of funding, very little work had been done to evaluate the effectiveness of educational interpreting. The UCLAN study was proposed specifically to enable researchers to look in more depth at the interaction of those directly involved in the lecturing/interpreting/learning process. The study had two strands, one of which was aimed at addressing the lack of awareness of the needs of deaf students within higher education, while the other investigated the effectiveness of interpreted classroom interaction.

To this end, the UCLAN study was interested in looking at much more than simply the activity of the interpreter. The different participants in an interpreted event, the power balance or imbalance between participants, the number of participants, the environment in which the event takes place, and the presence and use of other media in that environment can all have an effect on the interpreter's choice and use of language and on the extent to which he or she is able to work effectively. Similarly, the very presence of an interpreter can have an effect on any or all of the above (Wadensjö, 1998; Metzger, 1999; Harrington & Turner, 2000).

Cecilia Wadensjö (1998) suggests that, at the very minimum, there are three participants or groups of participants in an interpreted interaction. These are (a) minority language users, (b) majority language users, and (c) interpreters. In the UCLAN study, the participants included lecturers (both BSL users and English users), students (the majority of whom were English users, with the rest being BSL users), and people who were employed as note-takers, as well as the interpreters.

The research team was made up of two researchers, one a deaf BSL user, the other a Member of the Register of BSL-English interpreters (MRSLI).[1] During one academic year, they observed and filmed 32 hours of interpreted lectures. The data included examples of 15 different lecturers across eight subject areas: Education Studies, Deaf Studies, Social Work, Counselling, 3D Design, Business Management, Social Studies, and Computing. In these settings were 11 individual deaf students and nine different interpreters. Of the interpreters, four were MRSLI. Another three were experienced interpreters, each with at least three years of experience in interpreting, who were undergoing an approved Interpreter Training Program (ITP) and were registered with CACDP as trainee interpreters, but had not yet gained MRSLI status. The remaining two had advanced BSL skills and held certificates in sign communication skills, but had not undergone an approved ITP. Again, this study began with the assumption that the interpreter in any given event was competent and did not focus on an individual interpreter's skill, but upon the interpreted event as a whole.

By the nature of the languages involved in the UCLAN study, and other studies where one of the languages is a signed language, the gathering of video-recorded evidence is essential, since the only way one can capture, and later transcribe in detail, all aspects of the discourse that is observed, is by using both audio and visual media. Thus, in gathering data, the researchers used two VHS video cameras. These were positioned in such a way that they recorded the activity not only of the interpreter, but the lecturer, the students, both deaf and hearing, and the visual classroom environment. This was usually achieved by having the cameras positioned opposite each other, sometimes at either side of the classroom, sometimes at the front and back.

In addition, the researchers interviewed the participants, where possible, to find out (1) how they felt about the event, (2) whether they felt everyone participating in the event had equal access to the information being given, and (3) what, if anything, they would wish to change about the event. For the purpose of the interviews, hearing participants were interviewed by the hearing researcher, while the deaf researcher interviewed deaf participants. This ensured that everyone was offered the opportunity to be interviewed and respond in their first or preferred language.

Some participants were asked to watch parts of the videotapes and comment on what they observed. They were also asked whether, following discussion with the researcher, their opinion of the event, or of a particular part of the event, had changed as a result.

In the course of the study, several variations in terms of the numbers of participants and their roles in the event were observed, as follows:

1. One English-speaking, hearing lecturer with one deaf (BSL) student, a number of hearing students, and one hearing, bilingual (BSL/English) interpreter
2. One English-speaking, hearing lecturer with two or more deaf (BSL) students, a number of hearing students, and one hearing, bilingual (BSL/English) interpreter
3. One bilingual (BSL and English) lecturer with one deaf (BSL) student, a number of hearing students, and one hearing, bilingual (BSL/English) interpreter
4. One bilingual (BSL and English) lecturer with two or more deaf (BSL) students, a number of hearing students, and one hearing, bilingual (BSL/English) interpreter
5. One deaf (BSL) lecturer with one deaf (BSL) student, a number of hearing students, and one hearing, bilingual (BSL/English) interpreter
6. One deaf (BSL) lecturer with two or more deaf (BSL) students, a number of hearing students, and one hearing, bilingual (BSL/English) interpreter
7. One deaf (BSL) lecturer with one deaf (BSL) student, a number of hearing students, and two hearing, bilingual (BSL/English) interpreters

Each combination of these variations in the number and type of participants taking part in a particular classroom situation contributed to the creation of a different dynamic. For example, where there was only one deaf student, the interaction between that student and other people in the room was less frequent than in situations where there were two or more deaf students. In the latter case, the deaf students had the opportunity to discuss issues with each other as they arose, which tended to lead to more questions being asked by them of the lecturer. These logistical factors, as well as sociolinguistic factors, constitute the major findings of this study, and these are described in the next section.

FINDINGS

Analysis of the data provided information related to both logistical effects on the interaction between deaf and hearing participants and to sociolinguistic factors such as turn exchanges. The sociolinguistic factors are identifiable from the transcript itself. The logistical factors relate to such variables as the number of either the deaf students or the interpreters in a classroom.

LOGISTICAL EFFECTS

A variety of logistical factors had an impact upon the interpreted events under investigation. These included the number of deaf students; the number of hours worked by a single interpreter with no breaks; the number of interpreters working at a particular event; and the size, acoustics, lighting, and desk arrangements in the rooms themselves.

Number of Deaf Students

The presence of two or more deaf students in the classroom often affected the nature of the interpreting process. If the deaf students were signing to each other, unlike their hearing peers, they were unable to continue to follow the lecture at the same time. In saying this, the researchers are not claiming that hearing students can both socialize and attend to a lecture simultaneously. Rather, they are suggesting that while hearing students can talk with their peers and still monitor the lecture to at least some extent, deaf students could not. This would be because hearing is a passive task, which is not particularly directional, whereas looking is an active task, which is directional. If one student looks at another, he or she cannot also look at an interpreter (Winston, 1990; 1994; 2004 [in press]). This left the interpreters with a dilemma. Should they continue interpreting, knowing that the students were missing potentially vital information, or should they attempt to store the information being imparted by the lecturer and summarize it when the students completed their own discussion? Some interpreters chose to continue interpreting; some stopped interpreting until the deaf students returned their attention to the lecture, at which point they were given a summary of what they had missed. On one occasion, the interpreter stopped interpreting, waved to gain the attention of the students, and, having done so, continued with interpreting. Among the various interpreters observed, there did not appear to be any consistent rationale for these choices—rather it appeared that each interpreter, at a given moment, reacted to unique sets of circumstances. As Metzger and Fleetwood (forthcoming) point out, choices such as these could be guided by a clearly defined standard of practice if the interpreter's goal has been clearly identified. For example, the interpreter faces numerous options, including but not limited to:

1. continue interpreting and take no other action
2. continue interpreting and summarize what was missed
3. continue interpreting but try to gain the students' attention at every opportunity
4. continue interpreting, alert the student whenever the discourse includes items that would likely take the attention of the student(s) if they were hearing (e.g., if their name is called, if the word test is used, etc.)
5. stop interpreting and wait for the student(s) to watch the interpreter, then resume interpreting from that point
6. stop interpreting and when the students look again, summarize what was missed
7. stop interpreting, but try to gain the students' attention at every opportunity
8. stop interpreting, but alert the student whenever the discourse includes items that would likely take the attention of the student(s) if they were hearing (e.g., if their name is called, if the word test is used, etc.)

   (adapted from Fleetwood & Metzger 1990)

Each option achieves different results. Clearly, in terms of observed practice, there is currently no one strategy for dealing with this. When subsequently debated with groups of interpreting students, this particular issue has raised a number of interesting questions. One in particular that comes up regularly in such discussions is the question of who is responsible for the deaf student's learning. Some will argue that the interpreter is responsible for ensuring that deaf students do not miss any important information, while others will argue that deaf students, like any others, have the right to "not listen" in the classroom. Further research regarding the outcomes of these options on the educational, social, emotional, and intellectual experience of deaf students would allow practicing educational interpreters to serve their students more effectively, and would allow ITPs to better prepare interpreting students for the challenges of interpreting in classrooms.

Number of Hours Worked and Number of Interpreters

Only one interpreter provided interpreting services in almost all of the events that were observed and recorded, most of which were scheduled for at least two hours. It was usual for the lecturer to take a short break after the first hour, but some of the interpreters we observed were working for up to six hours in a day. There was some evidence from some of the videotaped data to suggest that interpreters who were observed and recorded both in morning and afternoon lectures appeared *to cope better and interpret more effectively* earlier in the day.

In some of the observed events where there were two interpreters, the co-working strategies that were employed varied quite significantly. In one instance where the lecture was being given by a deaf lecturer, and there was one deaf student in the class, one interpreter sat at the back of the room, interpreting the lecture into spoken English, while the other sat at the front of the room, interpreting into BSL what was said by hearing students, and into spoken English what was signed by the deaf student. It became particularly clear that the interpreters were not working effectively as a team at points where the deaf student and the lecturer were addressing each other. The two interpreters were working with different processing times, while the student and the lecturer were signing to each other without any awareness of this. The result was that the two interpreters found themselves speaking over each other, with the answer to a student's question often coming before the question had been voiced, or at the same time. Suffice to say, the hearing students found it somewhat difficult to follow what was being said.

Again, this is an example of an area for further research. If data-based research can assist in identifying which co-working practices work best in particular situations, working interpreters will be better able to improve services and ITPs will be better able to improve training methods for interpreting students. Even from this project, having observed a number of different co-working practices, there was an opportunity to take this topic back into the classroom and explore it with student interpreters. As a direct result of this project, specific training on co-working strategies now makes up a significant portion of one of the modules a student must complete before earning the UCLAN postgraduate diploma in BSL-English interpreting. (See Shaw [2000] for further discussion of team interpreting.)

Environmental Factors

On another point, during the course of this study, several different teaching rooms were used. Some were too small, others too large; some had poor lighting or poor acoustics; and some had fixed seating and desks. The effects of these different environments on the whole interpreted education process were sometimes quite negative. For example, one interpreter working in a room with poor acoustics found the task much more difficult, since, as Cokely (1992) has pointed out, to interpret effectively, one has to be able to hear what is being said. Again, the use of technical equipment such as overhead projectors, televisions, and videos sometimes impacted on the students' ability to take in information, and on the interpreter's ability to function effectively. Winston (1990; 1994; 2004 [in press]) and Johnson (1991) highlight this issue, making the point that a Deaf student can only take in one mode, visual information, whereas hearing students are often expected to take in two, managing both visual and acoustic input. The project data suggests that the interpreters being observed also had difficulties in dealing with multimedia, particularly when their process time was such that the materials to which they were about to refer had already been removed from sight by a lecturer who had finished referring to them (an instance of this can be seen later, in example 3). Research regarding the different strategies interpreters can use in such situations would allow for more professional interpreters and more students of interpretation to use effective strategies quickly so that students would not be subject to missed information.

SOCIOLINGUISTIC FACTORS

Sociolinguistic issues found in the data include overlapping speech, language choice, and the effects of the environment on the interaction. The following transcriptions and analyses provide three examples of these, taken from the study data. The first example relates to how language is used and manipulated in the classroom. It shows an interpreter presented with overlapping speech and provides an opportunity to observe the effects that processing time can have on the way in which an utterance might be understood, or misunderstood. The second highlights the importance of comprehension and language choice in ensuring clarity of interpretation. The third shows how the environment, other media, and a lack of awareness on the part of others regarding the interpreter's role can affect the extent to which an interpreter can be effective.

Example 1: Overlapping Speech

This first example is 30 seconds in duration and was taken from a lecture given by a hearing lecturer, bilingual in spoken English and BSL, in a classroom where there were two deaf students, a number of hearing students, and one hearing, bilingual (BSL/English) interpreter. The subject was Deaf Studies. The lecture, being delivered to students in the second year of their undergraduate degree program, had been in progress for 32 minutes. The names of the two deaf students have been changed. (A key to the transcription can be found at Appendix 1.)

This excerpt was chosen because it is one of several examples that demonstrate the potential for misunderstanding that can occur even when the communication process itself seems to be working quite well.

The first utterance (1.1) is from the lecturer, followed at a fairly short processing time (fractionally over two seconds) by the interpreter, whose BSL interpretation is glossed in uppercase in the transcription. As this short excerpt begins, the lecturer poses a question that is directed at the two deaf students (1.1–1.3). Before the lecturer finishes posing this question, one of the other students interrupts and speaks over the lecturer (1.2–1.4). This interruption leads the lecturer to make another statement (1.4), and all of this has occurred before the interpreter has finished posing the initial question to the deaf students:

1.1
(Lecturer) I   mean . . I   don't know if John and Mary . . want to
                                    (Interpreter) PRO.1 DON'T KNOW

1.2
comment   whether   they   think . . .   their   lives   are   different . . . .
I-F   MARY   JOHN   WANT SAY SOMETHING . . .   I-F SELF   FEEL   YOUR
     (ns - gaze) (ns - gaze)   (PRO.2)
                                        (Hearing Student)   Yes   but

1.3
compared   with   the   previous   generations   of   Deaf   people . . .
     YOUR   LIFE   DIFFERENT . . .   COMPARE   PREVIOUS
     (PRO.2)
it still   seems to   be   going   round   in   circles   and   circles   and

172 : FRANK J. HARRINGTON

1.4
I   don't   know   whether   that's   true   really...
GENERATION   DEAF   PEOPLE   *Yes I think it is*
                                                    (pointing at Deaf Student #1)
circles.
          (Deaf Student #1) YES
                    (nodding for 1–2 sec)
1.5
I   mean   th~ there   have   been   great   changes   in   this   country
                                                    I   mean   it's
          SAME   CLOTHES   CHANGE   CHANGE   CHANGE   TECHNOLOGY
                                        (Deaf Student #2) YES
                                                    (nodding)
1.6
for   Deaf   people . . . .
like . . .   it's   like . . . .   as clothes change, technology's changed   and . . .
CHANGE   CHANGE   CHANGE . . .
     (nodding)   HOW   AGE   CHANGE . . .
1.7
and   age   has   changed.

The interpreter, in asking the question, has changed its form from an indirect question, which may not have required an answer, to a direct question, by the use of the repeated personal pronoun (1.2–1.3). When he subsequently voices the deaf student's reply (in the first person singular) (1.4), it is, coincidentally, spoken at precisely the moment when it could be taken by the other students and the lecturer to be a reply to the lecturer's subsequent statement, rather than to the original question. The potential for confusion is further compounded by the fact that the voiced reply (1.4) appears to be an appropriate, although somewhat negative, response to the lecturer's second statement.

If we isolate the spoken English utterances in this interaction, up to the point where the deaf student's first utterance is voiced, it reads as follows:

Lecturer: I mean, I don't know if John and Mary want to comment, whether they think their lives are different from previous generations of deaf people?

Student: Yes, but it still seems to be going round in circles and circles and circles.

Lecturer: I don't think that's true really . . .

Deaf student: Yes I think it is.

Anyone simply hearing this piece of interaction (without watching or understanding the BSL) could be forgiven for misunderstanding its meaning, and the fact that the deaf student's utterance appears to negate the lecturer's second statement could explain why the lecturer does not take more notice of it.

The lecturer, having replied to the hearing student, naturally wishes to continue clarifying his point (1.5–1.6), but elects not to do so while the interpreter is still voicing for the deaf student who has continued to answer the initial question (1.6–1.7).

The interpreter has taken a decision that has affected the course of subsequent events. By choosing to continue interpreting the lecturer's original question, he has automatically omitted the overlapping statement made by the other student (see Roy, 1989; 2000 for a discussion of interpreters managing overlapping talk and turn exchanges). Further, he voices the deaf student's response to that original question, but he does not interpret the lecturer's response to that overlapping statement (1.4). Thus, he halts the progress of that potential new strand of discussion by continuing to voice the deaf student's extended response to the first question.

Meanwhile, the deaf students are unaware that any other interaction, beyond the lecturer's original question, has been taking place. They are not aware that the subject has been changed or that the discussion has begun to move on, and as a result, the rest of the class is brought back to the deaf students' responses to the initial question.

At a first glance, this appeared to be a relatively successful moment in the interpreting process. One might suggest that no real harm has been done in this case, and, overall, the learning process has not been adversely affected by the situation. In fact, the interpreter's decision to continue with the original question, in itself dictated by the need to ignore the overlapping speech of the hearing student, and further compounded by the purely coincidental timing of particular utterances, has not only caused potential misunderstanding, but has dictated the way in which the subsequent interaction would go. One wonders whether the lecture would have been significantly different if the interpreter had interpreted the student's overlapping utterance instead of the end of the lecturer's initial question? This example supports Roy's (1989; 2000) findings that interpreters are not merely conduits to an interaction. More, it provides clear evidence that more research is needed to determine the potential effects of the interpreter's management of turn exchanges, so that interpreters might be better prepared to make those choices and/or to remedy them, if necessary.

Example 2: Language Choices

This second example is 24 seconds in duration and is taken from a lecture given by a hearing lecturer, bilingual in spoken English and BSL, in a classroom where there were five deaf (BSL) students, a number of hearing students, and two hearing, bilingual (BSL/English) interpreters. As with the first example, the subject was Deaf Studies, and the topic of the discussion was the variety of forms of medical intervention that are used in attempts to cure deafness. The lecture was being delivered to students who were in the second year of their undergraduate degree program and had been in progress for 35 minutes.

This example (again, one of a number of such examples observed in the project data) has been chosen to illustrate the difficulties that interpreters and deaf students face when an utterance is not fully understood, or when the way in which it needs to be explained is not clear. The implications of interpreting *meaning*, rather than *lexicon*, especially in this type of situation, where that which is being explained is completely outside the deaf students' experience, are particularly apparent here.

The example begins with the lecturer asking the class for further comments, at which point one of the students suggests that sound received through a cochlear implant is reported to sound "tinny" (3.1–3.2).

3.1
(Lecturer)   ok . . . mhm . . . . . anything else? . .
(Interpreter)   MORE (GIVE)   ALSO
                                 (rpt)   (rpt)
(Student 1)   What you hear is supposed to be
3.2
WHEN FINISH IMPLANT MEAN   HEAR   WHAT   LIKE (PARENTHESES)
very   tinny,   isn't   it?

3.3

T-I-N-N-Y   MEAN   SOUN~   T-I-N-N-Y   (SPIRAL AWAY FROM EAR)
         (lp - "so mean")   (lp - "sound")
(Deaf Student 1)   (eb-v, q)

3.4

                                                  mhm ok

MEAN   SOUND SO-SO   LIKE   HEAR   WHAT   PERFECT   NO
(lp - "so mean")   (frown)   (q)

3.5

    that says   tinny . .   anything else?

MEAN   HEAR   LIKE   SO-SO   T-I-N-N-Y   HEAR
          (frown)   (eb-v, lp "oo", breath in)

As in the case of the first example, it is again useful initially to look at an English translation of what is uttered by the interpreter in an attempt to get this concept across.

> Interpreter: Also, once the implant has been carried out, it means that what you hear is "tinny," that means . . . "tinny," that means it sounds so-so, like . . . what you hear isn't perfect, but just so-so . . . it sounds . . . "tinny" . . .

The first thing to notice here is the very short process time that is being allowed by the interpreter (fractionally over one second). It means that they are filling time with a self-generated utterance ("once the implant has been carried out...") until they have heard enough of what the student is saying to begin an interpretation. The second point is that the notion of "tinny"-ness is a specifically "hearing" notion. It describes a distinct type of metallic, distant, electronic sound associated with listening devices, such as telephone receivers, transistor radios, and the like.

Cokely (1992) suggests that the shorter the process time allowed by an interpreter, the more likely it is that the interpretation will take the form of Sign Supported English (SSE), rather than BSL. He gives a number of instances in which this might happen, and suggests, in particular, that this occurs when the interpreter has not understood what he or she heard. In this situation, it is not perhaps that the interpreter has not understood, but rather that she is not prepared for the comment that has been made. She focuses on the English word, which she fingerspells. Having done this, she is left with no option but to offer an extended interpretation that attempts to explain the notion of something "sounding tinny" to the deaf students. As a concept, the notion of something "sounding tinny" is most likely outside of the experience of the deaf students in the classroom, and the lack of comprehension on the part of at least one of them is evidenced by the frown that elicits a repetition of the fingerspelled word *tinny* (3.3).

In instances such as these, it may be much more important for the intent or meaning of a comment to be understood, as part of the learning process, rather than that a particular word is explained. When the researchers subsequently discussed this event with the interpreter, they explored alternative ways in which the intent of the original comment could be explained in BSL. One suggestion was that the interpreter create a visual metaphor that would be understood in BSL, rather than relying on the aural metaphor of spoken English, which relied upon an understanding of sound. Another suggestion was to simply find alternative signs that would give an impression of the lack of clarity or unnatural quality of the sound that is reproduced by a cochlear implant.

Interpreters make decisions about language choice every moment of every event they interpret. What makes this instance particularly interesting is the metalinguistic challenge of having to use a visual/gestural language to describe an aural experience, which is peculiar to users of an oral/aural language and is outside of the experience of the deaf students in this classroom. Once again, research regarding the ways in which interpreters handle these situations, and the effects of their choices on the outcomes of the interaction, could help provide practicing interpreters and interpreter educators with information that would ultimately improve the effectiveness of interpreting services.

Example 3: The Effects of the Environment on the Interaction

This third example is included here as it gives an example of the effects of the environment and the use of different media on the interpreted event. It is 29 seconds in duration and was taken from a lecture given by an English-speaking lecturer in a classroom where there were a number of hearing students, two deaf students, one interpreter, and one note-taker. The subject was Social Studies, and the lecture, being delivered to students in the first year of their undergraduate degree course, had been in progress for 12 minutes.

In this case, a transcript is given, along with a diagram, showing the way in which the classroom was set up and the positioning of the deaf students, the lecturer, the note-taker, and the interpreter (Figure 1).

As can be seen from Figure 1, the interpreter is sitting to the left of the lecturer at a desk that is opposite the two deaf students and the note-taker, who are to the lecturer's right. At the beginning of the lecture, the lecturer had placed handouts on the desk in front of the deaf students and the note-taker. These were passed around the room, finishing up in front of the interpreter. The lecturer did not keep a copy of the handout for herself, and as can be seen from the transcript, had to take a handout from in front of the interpreter.

At the beginning of the transcript, the lecturer begins a new sentence (4.1-4.2) and, at the same time, walks across in front of the interpreter to retrieve a copy of the handout while continuing to speak. The interpreter, having just begun to sign the first part of what is being said, finds her eye contact with the deaf students broken and stops signing until the lecturer has moved out of her way (4.2). The lecturer continues to speak and is now pointing to a particular section of the handout (4.3). The interpreter's process time has been further delayed by the loss of eye contact, and as she is about to direct the students' gaze towards the lecturer, the lecturer stops pointing at the paper and moves across the interpreter again to replace the handout on the pile from which it originally came (4.4). The lecturer continues to speak, with the delayed interpreter now working at an extended delay (4.5–4.6).

4.1
(Lecturer) At the end of last week, we .. looked at catchment areas of   schools . . . .

(Interpreter)   LAST WEEK END WE THOUGHT
                                                           (lp - "at the end")

4.2
. . .   so we're moving back to this handout, OK? . .
(moves across interpreter to pick up paper—moves back again)
ABOUT SCHOOL . . . .   BACK
          (gaze - follows lecturer . . . . .)

4.3

and we looked at catchment areas of schools, which is three four . .

THIS PAGE WE LOOK (POINT) DIFFERENT SCHOOL (PLACE) . . . THIS

(lp - "handout") (v right)

4.4

right . . . .   and we

    (moves across interpreter to put paper back on table—moves back again)

SECTION 3.4 ABOU~   ABOUT

      (gaze—follows paper as lecturer puts it down on table)

4.5

talked about in the education reform act parents could make a choice about

SCHOOL (PLACE) AREA (PUT IN - POINT)   UNDER EDUCATION

               (rpt) (lp - "so")

4.6

where they sent their kids   and   the   impact   that   had

   CHANGE   A-C-T MEAN   SHOULD SAY PARENTS HAVE CHOICE

  (lp - "reform")

There are several points that can be drawn from this final example. The first relates to physical obstruction of sight lines. It is clear that any obstruction to the sight line between the students and the interpreter will have an effect on the interpretation. In this instance, the interpreter's flow was interrupted twice, and she had to stop each time until her line of sight was cleared. The lecturer, while causing the physical obstruction to the interpreter's line of sight, continued to speak. As a result, the interpreter had to process and hold a greater-than-usual amount of information, and as the delay between the lecturer's utterances and her interpretation increased, her effectiveness in passing the message on to the deaf students was reduced. One particular point worth noting is the extent to which the interpreter relies upon English lip patterns (4.1, 4.3, 4.5). It may not be the case every time, but it is does appear that at points where her concentration is broken, the interpreter reverts to a more English style of signing. Again, this relates to Cokely's (1992) point about comprehension and process, referred to in the discussion of example 2 above. During the project, the researchers saw a number of other instances where sight lines were impaired. On two occasions, the lights were switched off without warning, but in most cases, the obstruction was caused by the movement of another person between the interpreter and the student.

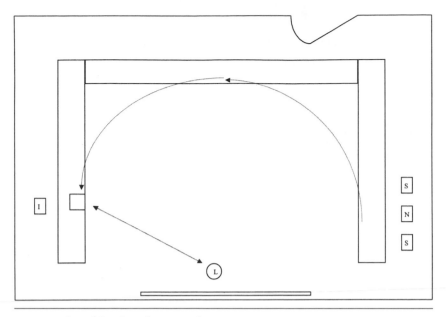

FIGURE 1. *Social Studies classroom layout*

I = Interpreter
N = Note-taker
S = Deaf Students
L = Lecturer

The second point that arises here relates to the simultaneous use of different media in the classroom. The project team regularly observed lecturers and students using overhead projectors, PowerPoint presentations, flipcharts, and whiteboards, often using more than one of these and other media simultaneously. In this instance, the second medium being used is the handout. While the other students in the classroom can listen to the lecturer and look at both her and the handout, the deaf students are not able to look at the interpreter, the lecturer, and the handout simultaneously. As a result, they are bound to miss something of what is being said or demonstrated. Again, see Winston (1990; 1994; 2004 [in press]) for an in-depth discussion of this situation as it relates to interpreting for deaf students in hearing classrooms. Here it is the specific part of the handout to which the lecturer is referring that is missed, and while this may not be particularly significant, it clearly makes life in the classroom less clear for these students. One area for future research would be to determine what strategies interpreters might be able to employ to compensate for this distinction.

The next point relates to the previous two, addressing the extent to which the lecturer is aware of the needs of the interpreter and the deaf students in her classroom. The interpreter needed to have sight of the students, the students needed to have time to take in the information simultaneously presented in different media, and it would have taken very little for the lecturer to plan things in such a way that these two needs could have been met. When lecturers were presented with examples such as this one by members of the project team, they often remarked that they had been completely unaware that there had been any disruption to the communication at the time. Again, with hindsight, they agreed that it would be appropriate to find ways of avoiding such unnecessary interruptions. Interpreters do have some options in terms of moving around the classroom while working or providing information to both hearing and deaf consumers about their needs as a professional service provider. Once again, further research might make clear the extent to which, and the appropriate strategies with which, interpreters might facilitate a solution to such situations.

One final point that came from this example was that it reinforced for the project team the importance of taking account of all available information when carrying out a project of this kind. When the researchers first looked at this example, they began by watching the videotape that only showed the interpreter. They were unable to understand why the interpretation became so disjointed at this particular point or why the interpreter was leaving such long gaps. It was only when the other tape, showing the actions of the lecturer, was viewed, and the tapes were subsequently viewed together, that they began to understand the extent to which other factors were affecting the interpretation. Clearly, without taking into account the environment, the other participants, and their effect on the interpretation, a researcher could potentially have identified this event as an example of dysfunctional interpreting. Taking a broader view of events enables us to determine the extent to which both linguistic and nonlinguistic aspects of an event can affect the message and the accessibility of that message to those relying upon the interpreter for their education.

CONCLUSIONS

Demonstrating the need for all participants to develop their awareness of the roles of others, and the need to negotiate interaction and relationships in the classroom, became two of the fundamental outcomes of the project. While one strand of the project was analyzing videotaped data and developing new ideas to be incorporated into the training of interpreters, the other strand was putting into practice some of these most practical findings by developing and delivering awareness training for lecturers and students.

The examples given show a variety of factors that can affect any interpreted event. They also show that in any event, all of these factors have an equal role to play in defining whether the event will ultimately be successful or not. In viewing the data, the research team became aware that multiple factors, identified in the examples above (both logistic and sociolinguistic factors), rarely came together in a single event. However, on the few occasions when they did, the outcome was a complete (if momentary) breakdown in the communication process. The project team concluded that the best way of reducing the occurrence of this situation was to ensure that all participants involved in interpreted classroom events were aware of their roles and the roles of others. This supports the findings of Metzger (1995; 1999), which suggest that while all the participants in an interpreted encounter may frame the event as an interpreted encounter, each participant's understanding of what makes up an interpreted encounter can impact upon the way that it unfolds.

This study was one of the first steps to be taken in the U.K. to look more closely at interpreters in some of the complex social situations in which they find themselves every day. Some of the outcomes of the study were both predictable and practical, redefining the ways in which interpreters, lecturers, and students relate to, and work with, each other in a higher education institution. Some of the events that were observed raised issues which are not solely relevant to educational interpreting, but which can apply to interpreting in a variety of settings, and the discussion of which can be of use to both interpreting students and those responsible for their training.

Studies of this nature are most important if interpreting and interpreter education pedagogy are going to continue to develop. Training exists in order to equip interpreters to work effectively and ethically with those who use their services. But this education may be seriously flawed if it is based only on hypothesis and anecdotal evidence. Studies that observe and describe what it is that interpreters actually do when they are interpreting can help interpreter educators to understand the complex nature of various settings in which interpreters work, and can provide invaluable information for them, supporting hypotheses with real-life examples. The more one can observe interpreters in real settings, the more knowledge one will have about the complexity of the interpreter's task. Educators with such knowledge will be better able to continually modify and improve the training they offer to their students.

In addition to the direct benefits of training, there are particular benefits to this type of research for those interpreters directly involved in the study. One of the underlying principles of this study is that research is carried out for the benefit of those who are stakeholders. Among these stakeholders are the interpreters who are being observed. Data captured on videotape, which can be analyzed and commented upon in detail, can be invaluable to the education and development of not only interpreting students, but interpreters themselves.

Mason (2000) has suggested that, in interpreting research such as this, there is a real need to take into account the part played by posture and eye gaze. Clearly the benefits of video recording could be enjoyed by those researching spoken language interpretation as well as by those researching signed language interpretation. There are clear advantages in using videotaped data, not least because they enable researchers to access both the verbal and nonverbal, or manual and nonmanual, information that is present. This also extends to environmental information. So, by filming a particular event, a sighted, hearing researcher, competent in the languages being recorded, can subsequently observe the available linguistic information, as well as the positioning of participants, whether they are standing or sitting, their relative proximity to each other, and so on.

Beside all of this, the study gave researchers an opportunity to begin to look at how language is understood, used, and manipulated by BSL-English interpreters. There is a need for much more work of this nature to be undertaken; but at least this project, and others like it, has made a start.

ACKNOWLEDGMENTS

I gratefully acknowledge the support of colleagues at the University of Central Lancashire, in particular Graham H. Turner, Alan Hurst, Kyra Pollitt, Anji Gregg, Martin Atherton, and Noel Traynor, whose collaborations on other papers and presentations related to this and other studies have helped to develop and inform my understanding of this topic.

NOTES

1.   When this study was carried out, interpreters in England, Wales, and Northern Ireland became both registered and qualified through a series of language and interpreting skills assessments administered by the Council for the Advancement of Communication with Deaf People (CACDP). CACDP were the awarding body for the qualification, and also the organization that administered the register. There were two categories of registration: Member of the Register of BSL/English Interpreters (MRSLI) and Registered Trainee Interpreter (RTI).

More recently the system has changed. MRSLI status can now be gained through a variety of qualifications, including National Vocational Qualifications (NVQ) and recognized university programs. CACDP is the awarding body for the NVQ, but the register is now administered by an independent registration panel.

REFERENCES

Berk-Seligson, S. (1990). *The bilingual courtroom: Court interpreters in the judicial process*. Chicago: University of Chicago Press.

Brennan, M. (1976). Can deaf children acquire language? *Supplement to the British Deaf News*, 6 (2).

Brennan, M. & Brown, R. (1997). *Equality before the law: Deaf people's access to justice*. Durham, NC: Deaf Studies Research Unit, University of Durham.

Brennan, M., Colville, M. D., & Lawson L. K. (1980). *Words in hand: A structural analysis of the signs of British Sign Language*. Edinburgh: Moray House.

Brennan M. & Hayhurst, A. B. (1981). The Renaissance of BSL. In C. Baker and R. Battison (Eds.). *Sign language and the deaf community*. Silver

Spring, MD: National Association of the Deaf.

Cameron, D., Frazer, E., Harvey, P., Rampton, B., & Richardson, K. (1992). *Researching language: Issues of power and method*, London: Routledge.

Cokely, D. (1992). *Interpretation: A sociolinguistic model*. Burtonsville, MD: Linstok Press.

Fleetwood, E., & M. Metzger (1990). *Cued Speech transliteration: Theory and application*. Silver Spring, MD: Calliope Press.

Gile, D. (1995). *Basic concepts and models for interpreter and translator training*. Amsterdam: John Benjamins.

Harrington, F. J., and Turner, G. H. (2000). *Interpreting interpreting: Studies and reflections on sign language interpreting*. Coleford, UK: Douglas McLean.

Higher Education Funding Council for England (1996). *Access to higher education: Students with learning difficulties and disabilities*. A report on the 1993–4 and 1995–6 HEFCE special initiatives to encourage widening participation for students with disabilities. Bristol, England: HEFCE.

Johnson, K. (1991). Miscommunication in interpreted classroom interaction. *Sign Language Studies, 70* (Spring).

Kyle, J. G. (1978). The study of auditory deprivation from birth. *British Journal of Audiology, 12,* 37–39.

Kyle, J. G. (1979). Measuring the intelligence of deaf children. *Bulletin of British Psychological Society, 33,* 30–32.

Kyle, J. G. (1980). Auditory deprivation: A clarification of some issues. *British Journal of Audiology, 14,* 30–32.

Kyle, J. G., & Woll, B. (1983). *Language in sign: An international perspective on sign language*. London: Croom Helm.

Kyle, J. G., & Woll B. (1985). *Sign language: The study of deaf people and their language*. Cambridge: Cambridge University Press.

Mason, I. (Ed.). (1999). Dialogue interpreting. *The Translator: Studies in Intercultural Communication, 5* (2), 147–160.

Mason, I. (2000). *Models and methods in dialogue interpreting research.* Keynote paper presented at the Research Models in Translation Studies Conference, Manchester, England.

Metzger, M. (1995). The paradox of neutrality: A comparison of interpreters' goals with the realities of interactive discourse. *Dissertation Abstracts International, 57* (02), 663. (UMI No. 9620304)

Metzger, M. (1999). *Sign language interpreting: Deconstructing the myth of neutrality.* Washington, DC: Gallaudet University Press.

Napier, J. (2002). *Sign language interpreting: Linguistic coping strategies.* Coleford, England: Douglas-Mclean.

Pollitt, K. (1997). The state we're in: Some thoughts on professionalisation, professionalism and practice among the UK's sign language interpreters.

Deaf Worlds 13 (3), 21–27.

Roy, C. B. (1989). A sociolinguistic analysis of the interpreter's role in the turn exchanges of an interpreted event. *Dissertation Abstracts International, 50* (11), 3573. (UMI No. 9009829)

Roy, C. B. (2000). *Interpreting as a discourse process.* Oxford: Oxford University Press.

Shaw, R. (2000). Team interpreting: A joint venture. *CIT News 20* (3).

Turner, G. H. & Harrington, F. J. (2000). Power and method in interpreting research. In M. Olohan, (Ed.), *Intercultural faultlines.* Manchester, UK: St. Jerome Publishing.

Wadensjö, C. (1992). *Interpreting as interaction: On dialogue interpreting in immigration hearings and medical encounters.* Linköping, Sweden: University of Linköping.

Wadensjö, (1998). *Interpreting as interaction.* London: Longman.

Winston, E. A. (1990). Mainstream interpreting: An analysis of the task. In L. Swabey (Ed.), *Proceedings of the eighth national conference of Interpreter Trainers.* N.p.: CIT.

Winston, E. A. (1994). An interpreted education: Inclusion or exclusion. In R. C. Johnson & O. P. Cohen (Eds.), *Implications and complications for deaf students of the full inclusion movement.t* (Occasional paper 94-2). Washington, DC: Gallaudet Research Institute.

Winston, E. A. (2004). *Language myths of an interpreted education.*Paper presented at the Supporting Deaf People Online Conference.

Winston, E. A. (in press). Interpreted education, classrooms and teachers. In E. A. Winston (Ed.), *Educational interpreting: How it can succeed.* Washington, DC: Gallaudet University Press.

Transcription symbol guide

The transcriptions at example 1 and example 2 have been made using the following conventions:

.. noticeable pause or break in rhythm.

... half-second pause.

.... one-second pause.

..... second and a half pause, and so on.

/?/ transcription impossible.

?—? utterance not understood.

Lowercase = spoken English

Lowercase *italicized* = English voicing of BSL

Lowercase (*italicized*) = nonverbal actions

SMALL CAPS = Gloss of BSL

~ = word not completed or completely uttered

Nonmanual Markers

lp = lip pattern

eb = eyebrows

^ = up

v = down

PRO.1 = First person

PRO.2 = Second-person possessive pronoun

ns = name sign used

gaze = eye contact with the subject

q = question

Contributors

Lawrence Forestal
  Senior Lecurer
Department of Speech and
  Hearing Science
Arizona State University
Tempe, AZ

Frank J. Harrington
Deaf Studies Team
Department of Education and
  Social Science
University of Central Lancashire
Preston, England

Maree Madden
Principal
Thomas Pattison School
New South Wales, Australia

Susan Mather
  Associate Professor
  Department of Linguistics
Gallaudet University
Washington, DC

Shaun Tray
Freelance Interpreter
Columbia, MD

Index

accreditation
  at advanced interpreter level, 5, 8,
    10
  of Australian interpreters. *See*
    National Accreditation
    Authority for Translators and
    Interpreters (Australia)
  certification of interpreters, 71, 76
  of professional signed language
    interpreters, 4, 13
acoustics in classrooms, 171
activities of daily living and OOS,
    32–33
advanced interpreter level accredi-
    tation, 5, 8, 10
A-Gaze. *See* Audience Gaze
age and attitudes of deaf leaders, 71,
    81, 83, 85, 86
AIIC (International Association of
    Conference Interpreters), 4
American Sign Language (ASL)
  euphemisms in, 110
  indirectness and, 109–11, 129
  innuendo and, 111–13, 129
  morphemes in poetry of, 111
  punning in, 111–13, 123, 129
  sign play in, 111–13
  taboo topics and, 110
  wit in, 111
aphorisms, 96
Armstrong, Michael, 145
asking and eliciting answers from
    students in interpreted classes,
    150–52
ASL. *See* American Sign Language
ASLIA. *See* Australian Sign Language
    Interpreters Association
assignment mix for interpreters, 58,
    61
attention-getting

"not listening" by deaf students in
    classroom and interpreter's
    response, 168–69
regulators in interpreted settings,
    148–50
strategies in interpreted classes,
    147–48
summoning strategies, 138
attitudes of clients toward interpret-
    ers, 11–12, 87–88
attitudes of deaf leaders toward
    interpreters, 71–91
  age and, 71, 81, 83, 85, 86
  attitude scale analysis, 80–81
  comparison of respondents, 78–
    80, 84–85
  deliminations, 75
  demographic information, 73
  educational level and, 82, 83, 85,
    86, 87
  experience with interpreters, 73,
    76–78, 81–82, 83, 85, 86
  findings, 75
  future research recommendations,
    87–89
  gender and, 82, 83
  larger sample analyses, 84–85
  limitations of study, 86
  methodology of study, 72–74
  negative experience and, 77, 81–
    82, 83–84, 85, 86
  population and sample, 74–75, 85
  reliability analysis, 74
  research question results, 83
  sample description, 75–76, 85
  statements of attitudes, 73–74
  supplementary analysis, 83–84
attitudes of women workers, 22
Audience Gaze (A-Gaze), 139, 140,
    147–48, 155–56, 157, 158

auditory deprivation in children, research on, 162

aurally oriented classrooms, 141–43, 148–50, 151

Auslan. *See* Australian Sign Language

Australia and Occupational Overuse Syndrome. *See* Occupational Overuse Syndrome (OOS)

Australian Association of the Deaf, 13

Australian Bureau of Statistics on wage gap for women, 21–22

Australian Sign Language (Auslan). *See also* Occupational Overuse Synddrome (OOS)

  accreditation in, 4–5

  interpreting into spoken English and from spoken English into Auslan, 6

  state and private agencies for interpreters of, 15

Australian Sign Language Interpreters Association (ASLIA), 5–6, 13, 35, 60, 63

backchanneling, 137

Baker, C., 137

Bammer, G., 31–32, 33

Barbe, K., 107

Bellugi, U., 111–12

benefits of employment and interpreters, 8, 14

Berk-Seligson, S., 164

Bienvenu, MJ, 112

Blignault, I., 31–32, 33

bluntness and Deaf people, 109–10

booking services for interpreters, 10, 15

Boreham, R., 22

bound morphemes, 103

Boxer, D., 107

Bristol University, 162, 163

British Sign language (BSL). *See* higher education classroom interpreting

Burg, A., 140–41

burn out in employment, 17

bystanders, 127

CACDP. *See* Council for the Advancement of Communication with Deaf People

cancellation rules for interpreting jobs, 12

career aspirations and OOS, 48–51, 58

caring work and implications for employment, 23–28

casual employment, 17

catchphrases, 105

Cazden, C., 144

Centre for Deaf Studies at Bristol University, 162

certification of interpreters, 71, 76

cheaper alternatives to interpreters, 13

children. *See also* classrooms; education

  pediatric medical visits, 87

  research on auditory deprivation of, 162

children of deaf adults (CODAs) as interpreters, 73

Chippewa Indians and humor, 101

circumlocution, 96–97, 102

civil legal matter interpreting, 15

classrooms. *See also* education; higher education classroom interpreting; visually based regulators

  acoustics in, 171

  asking and eliciting answers from students in, 150–52

  attention-getting strategies in interpreted classes, 147–48

  aurally oriented, 141–43, 148–50, 151

  as culture settings, 141–44

  design and visual fields, 140–41

  discussions between deaf students during lecture interpreting, response to, 168–69 environmental factors in, 171–72, 178–84

equivalence and, 124–25

eye gaze in, 137, 139

group discussions in hearing classrooms, 152

interpreted discourse in, 140

interpreters in and OOS, 31

interpreters' placement within, 140, 152–55

layout of, 178, 179

lecture interpreting, 87–88

lecture observation, 155–56

lecturer's awareness of needs of student and interpreter, 181

mainstreaming issues in, 140, 150

"not listening" by deaf students in classroom and interpreters' response, 168–69

observed communicative events in, 155–58

OOS in, 29, 31

platform lecture observation, 158

regulators in, 138

seating arrangements in, 152–55, 156, 178, 179

technical equipment in, 172, 180–81

turn-taking mechanisms in, 137, 150–52

visually-oriented, 142–43, 148–50, 151

client attitudes toward interpreters, 11–12

CODAs as interpreters, 73

code of ethics of interpreters, 7, 23–24

Cokely, D., 172, 178, 181

colleagues in interpreting workplace, 6

Colston, H., 125

common law and interpreter injuries, 55

communal identity and humor, 101

communicative competence, 103–4, 126

competency of sign language interpreters, 88, 164

comprehension of lectures by interpreter, 171, 180

conduits or channels, interpreters as, 21

confidentiality and impartiality of sign language interpreters, 7, 23–24, 58, 88

conflict of cultural views on role of interpreters, 148

consumers
  attitudes toward interpreters, 87, 88
  education of, 25

contexualization cues, 103, 126

contingent workers, interpreters as, 8–9

continuation regulators, 138, 150

continuing education, 61

contracts for interpreters, 10, 13

control of interpreters' over their work, 9–14

conversational cooperation, 105

conversational inference, 99, 100

conversational joking, 98, 105–6, 107, 124

conversation and innuendo. See innuendo

cooperative Principle for conversations, 104–5

coping strategies of interpreters, 27

Cortes-Conde, F., 107

Council for the Advancement of Communication with Deaf People (CACDP), 162–63, 166

counseling appointment interpreting, 88

courtroom interpreting, 9, 88

co-working of interpreters, 26–27, 62, 63, 170

Creswell, J., 145, 146

criminal legal matter interpreting, 15, 27

culture in classrooms settings, 141–44

teacher and interpreters. *See*
visually based regulators
ethnography, 144–45
euphemisms in ASL, 110
evasion, 96
"events of special significance"
interpreting, 15
Ewan, C., 32
exaggeration and intonation in
signing and conversation, 107,
129
expectations
of clients of interpreters, 17–18
of hearing people in regard to
interpreters, 12
eye assessment, 138
eye gaze to regulate discourse. *See*
visually based regulators;
specific types of gaze
eye-level summoning strategies, 138

face-threatening acts, 107, 108, 126
family life, effects of OOS on, 31–32,
44–48
feedback, 137
figurative language, understanding
of, 125
Fine, G. A., 101–2, 106, 109
fingerspelling, 129
Fleetwood, E., 140, 150, 168–69
flexible specialization theory of up-
skilling of employees, 10–11
fragmenting of interpreting workforce,
14
frames and humor, 125, 128, 129
frame shifting, 102, 103, 105
frank language, 113
freelance interpreter work
Deaf societies and, 15
frequency of, 5, 7
isolation of interpreting workplace
and, 26–27
labor market or union representation of, 12
limitations of, 5, 8

OOS and, 52–53
undercutting in, 13
working day of, 10
Frishberg, N., 124
full-time employment of interpreters,
13
OOS and, 52–53, 59
future research recommendations
attitudes toward interpreters, 87–89
innuendo interpreting, 130

Gallaudet University, 114, 122, 145
gallows humor, 101
gender
attitudes of deaf leaders toward
interpreters, 82, 83
caring work and implications for
employment, 23–28
flexible specialization theory of up-
skilling of employees and, 10–11
humor and, 108, 109
OOS and, 53, 54
research implications of, 4
sign language interpreting and, 21
situation specific interpreting and,
88
women's work and, 11, 17–23
working-class women's labor, 18–19
work-related injuries and, 22, 65
Georgetown University, 145
G-Gaze. *See* group-inducing gaze
Gibbs, R. W., 107, 108
Gile, D., 163
Goffman, E., 96–97, 102–3, 127
Graham, H., 24
Grice, H. P., 104–5, 124
grievance procedures, 63
group discussions
in hearing classrooms, 152
observation of, 156–58
seating arrangements for, 153–54
group-inducing gaze (G-Gaze), 139–
40, 147–48, 157, 158
Gumperz, J. J., 99, 103–4, 124, 126,
137, 141

Hall, R., 22
hand dominance and OOS, 57
Harley, B., 22
Hay, J., 108–9
Health Care Interpreter Service
    (HCIS, Australia), 15
health-related interpreting services,
    15, 87–88
hearing (non-Deaf) clients' expecta-
    tions of interpreters, 18
Heath, S. B., 145
HEFCE (Higher Education Funding
    Council for England), 165
Hendricks, Jon, 150
Henry, R., 98
higher education classroom interpret-
    ing, 162–187
  data from study, 165–67
  effects of environment on interac-
    tion, 178–84
  environmental factors, 171–72
  findings of study, 167–68
  language choices, 175–77
  logistical effects, 168–71
  methodology of study, 163–64
  "not listening" by deaf students in
    classroom and interpreters'
    response, 168–69
  number of deaf students and, 168–
    69
  number of hours worked and
    number of interpreters, 170
  overlapping speech, 172–75
  sociolinguistic factors, 171–72
  theoretical framework, 163–64
Higher Education Funding Council
    for England (HEFCE), 165
holiday pay, 63
hostility and innuendo, 128
hours of work of interpreters. See
    working hours of interpreters
human services work, 23
humor. See also punning
  Chippewa Indians and, 101

Cooperative Principle for conversa-
    tions and, 104
  description by discipline of, 102–3
  discontinuity and, 102–3
  disparaging, 106
  duplicity and, 102–3
  exclusion and, 101
  frames, creating, 125
  gallows, 101
  gender differences in, 108, 109
  impact on conversations, 105–6
  inclusion and, 100–101
  incongruity and, 102–3
  innuendo and, 97–98, 113
  linguistics of, 97–98, 102–8, 109
  male-centric, 109
  revealed, 106
  rules for, 124
  sexual, 100, 109, 117–22
  sign play and, 109
  spontaneity and, 108
  as subversion, 101–2
Humphries, T., 111, 113
Hymes, D., 124, 126, 143–44

IDEA (Individuals with Disabilities
    Education Act), 71
idealism and interpreters, 25–26
identity display and conversational
    joking, 107
I-Gaze. See individual gaze
illocutionary force in indirect speech,
    99–100
incongruity and humor, 102–3
incongruity Resolution Model, 103,
    104
indirect communication, 96–97
indirectness, 96–97, 98–100, 102,
    109–11
Individual gaze (I-Gaze), 139, 147–48,
    155–56, 157–58
Individuals with Disabilities Educa-
    tion Act (IDEA), 71
Industrial Revolution and women's
    work, 18–19

National Technical Institute for the
Deaf, 33
NCI. *See* National Committee on
Interpreting
needs of interpreters, 26–27
negative eye gaze, 137
negative issues in the interpreting
situation, 25
negotiation, 107
neutrality of sign language interpreters, 23–24
NIC. *See* National Interpreter
Certification (NIC) program
Nichols, T., 16
non-bona fide communications, 104–5
nonwage benefits and interpreters, 8,
14
Norrick, N. R., 105, 124
NOSHSC (National Occupational
Health and Safety Commis-
sion), 28
notice for cancellation of interpreting
job, 12
NSW Ethnic Affairs Commission
(EAC, Australia), 15, 16

Obeng, S. G., 96–97, 102
observation of interpreters, 58. *See
also* classrooms
occupational health and safety (OHS)
issues
"Duty of Care" and, 55
early warning signs of, 55–56
fragmentation of work and, 14
outsourcing and casualization,
consequences of, 14–17
research of, 3
stress and, 27
training in, 16, 56–57, 59, 60–61
work-related injuries and gender, 22
Occupational Overuse Syndrome
(OOS), 3–70
aetiology, 28–31
age and gender distribution of
subjects, 37–38

career aspirations and, 48–51, 58
caring work and implications for
employment, 23–28
clinical features of, 28
content of job and, 58
definition of, 28
design of study, 34–51
effects of OOS, 31–33
employment status of subjects, 38–
39, 52–53
ergonomic equipment and, 57
family status of subjects, 39
first language status of subjects, 39
gender and work, 17–23, 53
guidelines needed for, 56
hours of work and, 53–54, 61–62
hypotheses of study, 33–34, 52–54
implications and recommendations,
54–65
job experience and exposure, 41–
43, 52–54
job tenure and, 43, 52
labor process of signed language
interpreters, 9–14
management style and structure
and, 59–60
other service condition matters
and, 62–65
outsourcing and casualization,
consequences of, 14–17
physical environment and, 57
post industrial society, 8–9
prevalence of medically diagnosed
OOS, 40–41
preventive strategies, 54–64
private life, effect on, 44–48
procedure, 34–36
recruitment and selection procedures and, 60
response rates and accreditation of
subjects, 37
stages of, 29
subjects, 37–39
symptoms of OOS, prevalence of,
41

Index : 197

training on, 56, 58, 60–61
warning signs for, 56
weakness in design, 36–37
work duration, 43, 44–48, 52
work of signed language interpreters in Australia, 4–7
OHS. *See* occupational health and
safety (OHS) issues
OOS. *See* Occupational Overuse
Syndrome
outsourcing
casualization and, 14–17
of interpreting, 15–16
overlapping-dyad, 126–27
overlapping signs, 112
overlapping speech, 171, 172–75

Padden, C., 111, 113
pain experienced by interpreters. *See*
Occupational Overuse
Syndrome (OOS)
paradigm for spoken language
interpreting, 163
paraprofessional interpreters, 4–5, 8,
10
parent-teacher conference interpreting, 88
part-time employment of interpreters,
5, 17, 38, 52–53, 59
pay for interpreters. *See* wages
pediatric medical visit, attitude
toward interpreter in, 87
peripheral systems use in expressing
information, 137
personal relationships and OOS, 44–
48
physical environment. *See* environmental factors
"play" cue, 103
"play on sign." *See* sign play
politicians and innuendo, 102
positive eye gaze, 137, 139
posture and eye gaze, 183
pre-industrial Europe, women's labor
in, 17–18

pre-initiation regulators, 138
pressures on interpreters, 27–28, 30
prevention of illness and injury, 16–
17, 54–64
Priester, Elmer, 111, *The Princess
Plays with Wood* (innuendo
study using), 114–15
private life and oos, 44–48
profession, interpreting as, 6, 60
prosody, 137
proverbs, 96
public speaking situations and oos,
29, 31
punning. *See also* humor; Jokes
aggression and, 106
ASL and, 111–13, 123, 129
defining, 96
research on, 97

Raskin, V., 104–5
rates of pay for interpreters. *See* wages
ratified unaddressed participant, 127
recruitment and selection procedures,
60
reframing, 103
registry of BSL-English interpreters,
162, 165
Registry of Interpreters for the Deaf
(RID), 71, 76, 85
regulators. *See* visually based
regulators
relevance in interpreted encounter,
126
Repetitive Strain Injury. *See* Occupational Overuse Syndrome
(OOS)
reporting OOS, 56–57, 64
research. *See* future research recommendations; *specific studies*
*Researching Language: Issues
of Power and Method*
(Cameron), 164
rest breaks, 61, 62, 64
restructuring, 8
revealed humor, 106

threatening. *See* face-threatening acts
Tilly, L. A., 18
timeliness in interpreting, 126
time off from work and OOS, 40–41
trade unions. *See* unions and signed
    language interpreters
training on OOS, 16, 56–57, 58, 60–
    61
transliteration, 88–89
turn-taking
    in classrooms, 137, 150–52
    interpreters and, 126
    regulators in signed discourse,
        136–40
two interpreters on lengthy assign-
    ments, 26–27, 62, 63

UCLAN (University of Central
    Lancashire) study. *See* higher
    education classroom
    interpreting
undercutting by freelance interpret-
    ers, 13
unions and signed language interpret-
    ers, 5, 12, 63–64
United Kingdom deaf community
    research. *See* higher education
    classroom interpreting
university employment of interpret-
    ers, 9. *See also* higher educa-
    tion classroom interpreting
University of Central Lancashire
    (UCLAN) study. *See* higher
    education classroom
    interpreting
unnamed classifiers, 129
up-skilling of employees, 10–11
urban working-class women's labor,
    18

value of interpreter's work, 11–12
verbal irony, 97, 102, 107
verbal parody, 98
Victorian Interpreting and Translat-
    ing Service (Australia), 16

videorecording and spoken language
    interpreting research, 183
visual fields and classroom design,
    140–41
visually based regulators, 136–61
    analysis of study, 146–58
    asking and eliciting answers from
        students in interpreted classes,
        150–52
    attention-getting regulators, 148–50
    attention-getting strategies, 147–48
    classroom lecture observation,
        155–56
    classrooms as culture settings,
        141–44
    group discussion observation, 156–58
    interpreted discourse, 140
    interpreters' placement within
        classrooms, 140, 152–55
    literature review, 136–44
    methodology of study, 144–46
    observed communicative events,
        155–58
    platform lecture observation, 158
    turn-taking regulators in signed
        discourse, 136–40
    types of regulators, 138
    visual fields and classroom design,
        140–41
visually-oriented classrooms, 142–43,
    148–50, 151
visual metaphors, 177
visual summoning strategies, 138
vocal qualifiers, 137
Vocational Rehabilitation Act of
    1973, 71
voice-to-sign mode interpreting, 6, 29
voluntary interpreting, 3–4, 13

Wadnesjö, C., 140, 163, 165
wages
    fairness in, 62–63
    holidays, 63
    payment by results basis for
        interpreters, 12

rates of pay for interpreters, 13
shift work and, 63
women vs. men, 21–22
warning signs for OOS, 56
Weiner, M., 138
Whitehouse, G., 22
Wilson, C., 152
Winston, E., 140, 171, 180
wit in ASL, 111–12. *See also* humor
Wolverhampton University, 163
women. *See* gender
workers' compensation, 63
  freelance interpreters and, 8
  gender differences in types of work
      and, 22
working hours of interpreters, 9–10,
      11, 12, 13
  OOS and, 53–54, 61–62
work intensification for interpreters,
      11, 14, 16, 27
Workplace Health and Safety Act
      (Australia), 55, 64
Workplace Health and Safety
      Committee, 59, 64
Workplace Health and Safety
      representative, 64
workstation design, 3

Zajdman, A., 107, 126–27